P9-CRV-209

STILL MORE
GAMES TRAINERS PLAY

STILL MORE
GAMES TRAINERS PLAY

EXPERIENTIAL LEARNING
EXERCISES

Edward E. Scannell
Arizona State University

AND

John W. Newstrom
University of Minnesota-Duluth

McGRAW-HILL, INC.

New York   St. Louis   San Francisco   Auckland   Bogotá
Caracas   Lisbon   London   Madrid   Mexico   Milan
Montreal   New Delhi   Paris   San Juan   Singapore
Sydney   Tokyo   Toronto

Library of Congress Cataloging-in-Publication Data

Scannell, Edward E.
      Still more games trainers play : experiential learning exercises /
Edward E. Scannell and John W. Newstrom.
          p.   cm.
      ISBN 0-07-046427-8
      1. Small groups. 2. Games. 3. Educational games.
4. Experiential learning--Problems, exercises, etc. I. Newstrom,
John W.   II. Title.
HM133.S314   1991
302.3' 4--dc20   91–8576
                                                                CIP

Copyright © 1991 by McGraw-Hill, Inc. All rights reserved.
Printed in the United States of America. Except as permitted
under the United States Copyright Act of 1976, no part of this
publication may be reproduced or distributed in any form or by
any means, or stored in a data base or retrieval system, without
the prior written permission of the publisher.

          6 7 8 9 0   MAL/MAL   9 7 6 5 4 3

ISBN 0-07-046427-8

The sponsoring editor for this book was Ted Nardin, the editing
supervisor was Fred Bernardi, and the production supervisor was
Pamela Pelton.

Printed and bound by Malloy Lithographing, Inc.

Like its two predecessors, this book
is dedicated to those countless friends,
colleagues and co-workers around the
globe who have helped us become better
facilitators--both personally and pro-
fessionally.

Thank you.

TABLE OF CONTENTS

Publisher's Note

Preface

About the Authors

Publisher's Note:

This book is one of three in a highly successful series compiled by the authors. The first, __Games Trainers Play__, appeared in 1980. Its success stimulated the development of a second book of entirely different "games" which were published in 1983 as __More Games Trainers Play__. Back by popular demand, the authors have created (with input from many experienced trainers) this third book in the series.

Users of the previous two books have found them to be invaluable aids to a wide variety of training situations. The books have received high praise from reviewers, and should be on every trainer's bookshelf.

PREFACE

Since the advent of our first book, <u>Games Trainers Play</u> and its sequel, <u>More Games Trainers Play</u>, it seems that the entire field of experiential learning has seen a surprising and fascinating reception. In brief, it seems to be the "in" thing.

When <u>Games Trainers Play</u> was published ten years ago, we knew we might receive some negative feedback from our senior mentors. Happily, that negativity was far overshadowed by the very positive response from tens of thousands of trainers around the globe. That continuing enthusiasm from our HRD colleagues now brings us the third in our series, <u>Still More Games Trainers Play.</u>

We're often asked "How did this all start?" Having conducted numerous "Train The Trainer" Workshops for the American Society for Training and Development, we became very much aware of the need for activities and exercises to supplement the instructional phase of the program. Collecting the dozens of "games" was an enjoyable experience. When it came time for its title, we spent considerable time in identifying words. Initially, we dismissed the "games" word because it could connote gimmicky or frivolous activity. We were of the opinion that training is serious business and such a "cutesy" title might negate the importance of our mission. However, we decided to go with it and are totally convinced we made the correct decision.

All of these exercises have been field-tested and are presented to our readers with the conviction they deliver as promised.

The Format for each game uses this outline:

TITLE
OBJECTIVE
PROCEDURE
DISCUSSION QUESTIONS
MATERIALS REQUIRED
APPROXIMATE TIME REQUIRED
SOURCE

Whenever possible, we have identified the primary source or contributor of the activity. Since many such games are generic, it was not always possible to locate such origination. While we appreciate the numerous friends and associates who have sent us items, we also accept responsibility if we have missed an earlier source.

A sincere and warm acknowledgement is given to Betty Norris and her co-worker Rachelle Maxwell for their dedication and expertise in their skillful treatment of scribbled notes, scratched-over manuscripts, etc., etc., and transforming them into a handsome piece of work.

Edward E. Scannell
John W. Newstrom

EDWARD E. SCANNELL

A member of the National Speakers Association, Edward E. Scannell has given more than a thousand presentations, seminars and workshops across the U.S. and in several foreign countries.

Actively involved in both civic and professional organizations, he has served on the Board of Directors of a number of groups including the Tempe Chamber of Commerce, the Arizona Business-Education Partnership, the American Society for Training and Development (ASTD), Meeting Planners International (MPI), and the National Speakers Association. He was the 1982 National President of ASTD and later served a two-year term as the Executive Chairman of the Board of the International Federation of Training and Development Organizations.

He has written or co-written seven books and over fifty articles in the fields of Human Resource Development, Communication, Creativity, Meeting Planning, and Management. Two of these books, __Games Trainers Play__ and __More Games Trainers Play__, are used by speakers, trainers, and meeting planners around the world.

A past president of MPI Arizona's Sunbelt Chapter and its 1986 "Planner of the Year," he was also MPI's International President in 1988-89. He is currently serving as a Trustee for the MPI Educational Research Foundation.

An active member of the National Speakers Association and the recipient of the 1985 President's Award, Scannell was the 1987-88 President of the Arizona NSA Chapter. He is 1991-92 National President of NSA.

Currently the Director of the University Conference Bureau at Arizona State University, Scannell taught at the A.S.U. College of Business and previously at the University of Northern Iowa.

In recognition of his activities, he is listed in several "Who's Who" directories, including __Leaders in Education, Personalities in the Midwest, Who's Who in the West, Dictionary of International Biography__, and __Men of Achievement__.

DR. JOHN W. NEWSTROM

Dr. Newstrom is a university professor, author, and consultant to organizations in the areas of training and supervisory development. He is currently a Professor of Human Resource Management in the School of Business and Economics at the University of Minnesota, Duluth, where he has taught since 1976. He has conducted training programs on a wide range of topics for organizations including 3M, Lakehead Pipeline, LTV Steel, Blandin Paper Co., Diamond Tool, Minnesota Power Co., Clyde Iron, City of Scottsdale, Armour-Dial, St. Luke's Hospital, and Greyhound Computer Corporation.

John has been active in the American Society for Training and Development (ASTD) since 1971, holding elective offices (e.g., Secretary, Vice-President, President) in the Valley of the Sun (Phoenix) and Lake Superior (Duluth) chapters. He has written nine articles for the __Training and Development Journal__ on such topics as needs analysis, evaluation, transfer of training, and unlearning. He serves on the Editorial Review Board for the __Journal of Management Development__ and as a reviewer for the new __Human Resource Development Quarterly__. He is the co-author of the widely acclaimed books __Games Trainers Play__ and __More Games Trainers Play__. He has co-authored four other books recently: __Windows Into Organizations__ (AMACOM), __The Manager's Bookshelf__ (Harper & Row); __What Every Supervisor Should Know__ (McGraw-Hill); and __Managing Transfer of Training__ (Addison-Wesley).

His involvement with national ASTD includes nine presentations to national conferences, service on the national Board of Directors, Budget and Finance Committee, Publishing Committee, Research Committee, National Awards Committee, Institutes Committee, Student Services Task Force, and as the lead instructor for the "Basics of Training" workshop, which he taught nationally for ASTD for seven years. His administrative experiences include roles as Chairperson of the Business Administration Department at the University of Minnesota-Duluth, Director of the Center for Professional Development, Acting Director of the Bureau of Business & Economic Research (ASU), and Chairperson of the Management Education and Development Division of the Academy of Management. He has also served on the Board of Directors of several community organizations in Phoenix and Duluth.

STILL MORE
GAMES TRAINERS PLAY

I.

CLIMATE

SETTING AND

ICEBREAKERS

EXPECTATIONS

OBJECTIVE: To help ensure that the stated objectives of the training session are in general concert with those of the participants.

PROCEDURE: At the beginning of the session, the trainer defines the objectives of that particular module of instruction. An overview of the session with the major points and subpoints of the session are then identified. The attendees are told that in order to make sure their individual objectives are "in sync" with those objectives already stated, they will be asked to jot down 2-3 items they are looking for in this session (they should use "Expectations" form copied from page 5). After they individually write out their own expectations, form groups of 3-4 people. After groups report their findings, these are summarized and recorded on flip charts.

As the individual or group responses are reported to the group, be certain to acknowledge each and every item. If the attendees were given an advance agenda of the topics, most of their expectations will likely fall into these already identified areas.

On occasion, a participant's need may surface that is outside the objectives or content of the program. If so, thank the individual or group for their need, but suggest that this particular topic is really outside the agenda. If the requested topic is one with which the facilitator has some experience, offer to spend time with the individual at break times to discuss. If it is outside the trainer's expertise, ask group if they can assist. In all likelihood, a colleague will happily respond.

**MATERIALS
REQUIRED:** Form as shown.

**APPROXIMATE
TIME REQUIRED:** 15-20 minutes.

SOURCE: Unknown.

3

MISTAKEN IDENTITIES

OBJECTIVE: To enable large groups to make new acquaintances.

PROCEDURE: As each person enters the room, randomly give him/her a name tag with someone else's name on it. Then ask him/her to circulate around the room and find the person with the name tag with his/her name on it and make a switch. Continue until at least half the group has the correct name tag.

MATERIALS REQUIRED: Name tags.

APPROXIMATE TIME REQUIRED: 10-15 minutes.

SOURCE: Unknown.

MY FAVORITES

OBJECTIVE: To warm up, loosen, and relax an uptight audience.

PROCEDURE: Distribute copies of the "Exercise in Self-Disclosure" presented on page 11.

      a.   Ask them to identify their favorite color, then list three words that describe it. (Example: Blue--cool, relaxing, and distant.)

      b.   Ask them to identify their favorite animal; then list three words that describe it. (Example: Tiger--strong, tense, dangerous.)

      c.   Ask them to name their favorite city; then list three words that describe it. (Example: New York--exciting, busy, refreshing.)

Then suggest that their answers to question #1 (color) provide clues to how other people view them; that their answers to question #2 (animal) provide clues to how they view themselves; and that their answers to question #3 (city) provide a portrait of how they feel about their sensuality.

DISCUSSION QUESTIONS: How do you feel about the results of this exercise?

To what degree might this exercise provide valid clues?

What are the risks and costs associated with using limited and indirect clues to categorize and describe people?

MATERIALS REQUIRED: Copies of "Self-Disclosure".

APPROXIMATE TIME REQUIRED: 5-10 minutes.

SOURCE: Roxanne Frederickson, Billings, MT.
Tyna Rush, Reno, NV.

AN EXERCISE IN SELF-DISCLOSURE

DIRECTIONS: Answer each of the following questions quickly, and then provide a concise explanation or rationale for each answer.

1. Name your favorite color: _____ .
   Describe it in three words.
   a.
   b.
   c.

2. If you could pose (safely) for a publicity picture at the San Diego Zoo with the animal of your choice, what would it be? _____
   Describe three characteristics of that animal:
   a.
   b.
   c.

3. My favorite city: _____ .
   Describe it in three words.
   a.
   b.
   c.

SIGN-IN PARTY

OBJECTIVE: To give attendees a chance to become acquainted with other participants.

PROCEDURE: At the opening (or preopening) social event of large scale association or corporate meetings, have 20-25 sheets of flip chart paper taped to walls around the room. (Make sure this has been OK'd by hotel staff and that pens won't bleed through paper). Premark sheets alphabetically, A, B, C, etc. Here attendees sign in alphabetically. They may simply write their names on the appropriate sheet or write a message or comment.

A variation of this would have names of states on flip chart paper whereon participants might sign their names and also their hometowns by the respective home states.

After at least 4-5 people have assembled at most of the stations, ask each subgroup to find out at least 3 things they all have in common.

MATERIALS REQUIRED: Flip chart paper, 25 marking pens or pencils.

APPROXIMATE TIME REQUIRED: 15 minutes.

SOURCE: Unknown.

PLAYING CARD MIXER

OBJECTIVE: To be used as a get-acquainted mixer in large (100+) groups.

PROCEDURE: As individuals enter the reception area or meeting room, they are handed a single playing card drawn randomly from 3-4 mixed decks. Their task is to assemble 3-4 other people to combine their cards for the best poker hand. The winning team is awarded an inexpensive prize.

APPROXIMATE TIME REQUIRED: 10-15 minutes.

MATERIALS REQUIRED: 3-4 decks of playing cards and nominal prizes (books, tapes, etc.).

SOURCE: Unknown.

THE CELEBRITIES

OBJECTIVE: To create an ice-breaking opportunity.

To ensure that all participants will get involved.

To encourage participants to develop good questioning and data-gathering/detective skills.

PROCEDURE: Brainstorm a list of famous people (and/or creatures, such as Mickey Mouse, Superman, or E.T.) sufficient to cover the number of expected participants. Celebrities might include famous singers, actors/actresses, politicians, business people, writers, musicians, etc. Names may be drawn from a variety of fields, or may all have a common thread connecting them. (Examples are: celebrities related to the nature of the group; all names starting with the same letter; or all people who were popular during a particular era.) In addition, if you personally know the participants in advance, you might decide to match the assignment of celebrity names to individuals who have a similar characteristic.

Write these names on stick-on or pin-on name tags.

When participants arrive (e.g., during a social hour or preconference coffee time), present them with their task (to identify who their celebrity is) by asking questions that can be answered "Yes" or "No" of other participants. Then fasten a name tag to their back and encourage them to mill around with other participants.

DISCUSSION QUESTIONS: What kinds of questions were most useful in identifying who your celebrity was?

Were non-verbal cues helpful in solving your task? Explain.

What did you learn about each other through this exercise?

MATERIALS REQUIRED: Name tags.

APPROXIMATE TIMEREQUIRED: 15-30 minutes, depending on size of group, physical space for movement, familiarity of participants with celebrity names, etc.

SOURCE: Karen Honey, Australia Post, Melbourne, Australia.
Barbara Crowell, Phoenix, AZ.

THE WHOLE ROOM HANDSHAKE

OBJECTIVE: To have participants meet at least half of the entire group.

PROCEDURE: Have group form into two large circles--one inside the other. Participants in the inner circle turn and face those in the outer ring, quickly introduce themselves and continually move to right. The outer circle rotates left and the inner circle rotates right until all participants meet eachother. (NOTE: This activity works best with groups of 100 or less.)

MATERIALS
REQUIRED: None.

APPROXIMATE
TIME REQUIRED: 10 minutes.

SOURCE: Maggie Bedrosian, The Synergy Group, Silver Spring, MD.

THE HUMAN SPIDER WEB

OBJECTIVE: To warm up a new group, and break down their inhibitions.

To provide an opportunity for participants to work as a team and explore the dimensions of teamwork.

PROCEDURE: Select (randomly) 6-8 volunteers from the larger group to participate in an exercise (for demonstration purposes), or divide the entire group into teams of 6-8 individuals. Have each group move to a location that allows them to stand in a small circle.

Instruct members of each group to extend their left hands across the circle and grasp the left hands of the other members who are approximately opposite them. Then have them extend their right hands across the circle and grasp the right hands of other individuals.

Inform them that their task is to unravel the spider web of interlocking arms without letting go of anyone's hands. They either will be timed (as a way to place pressure on them), or will be competing with other groups to see who finishes the task first.

**DISCUSSION
QUESTIONS:**   What was your first thought when you heard the nature of the task? (Probably: "This will be impossible!")

What member behaviors detracted (or could detract) from the group's success in achieving its goal?

What lessons does this exercise have for future team-building?

**MATERIALS
REQUIRED:**   None.

**APPROXIMATE
TIME REQUIRED:** 15 minutes, plus discussion time.

SOURCE: Susan Hennig, Green Bay, WI.

THE 30-SECOND MONOLOGUE

OBJECTIVE: To allow attendees at meal functions or other events to become better acquainted.

PROCEDURE: The activity is designed to be used at the start of weekly or monthly organization meetings. After all participants are seated at their luncheon or dinner tables, announce it is time for the "30-Second Monologue." Each person will tell those at their table anything about her/himself that s/he wants to (name, position, hobby, avocation, etc.) in a 30 second time frame. The Program Chairperson calls time after exactly 30 seconds, at which time the second person speaks. Continue for 3-4 minutes in 30-second intervals or until each person has had her/his chance for self-introduction. (NOTE: Each table handles only those seated at that table, i.e., individuals do not speak to the entire room.)

**MATERIALS
REQUIRED:**   None

**APPROXIMATE
TIME REQUIRED:** 5 minutes.

SOURCE: Deborah Dellis & Bobette Gordon, Arizona Sunbelt MPI Chapter.

TOMBSTONE PLANNING

OBJECTIVES: To encourage participants to open up and disclose something meaningful about themselves.

To encourage participants to circulate among other group members during breaks.

PROCEDURE: Provide everyone with tent cards (e.g., 5 x 8 index cards folded in half) and the opportunity to use a magic marker.

Have everyone print their name on the front side (this gives them the chance to write a nickname such as "Liz" instead of the formal "Elizabeth" which may have appeared on their registration materials.)

Now instruct everyone to "Design your own inscription for their future tombstone." This should be a brief phase, couplet, or limerick that in some way provides a commentary on their lives, their achievements, their character, or their relationships. Examples may range from a cryptic "Ted is dead," to the emotion-dripping statement that "I told you I was sick, George!"

Now move on to your normal agenda for the session, reminding participants that they may roam around the room during refreshment breaks to inspect others' tombstone inscriptions.

DISCUSSION QUESTIONS: What inscriptions most caught your attention? What are they telling you?

If you now had the chance to design a new inscription, what would it be? (Note: In a two-three day workshop, you may wish to give people the chance to "wipe their slates clean" every day, and send new signals to their co-trainees.)

MATERIALS REQUIRED: Tent cards and magic markers; perhaps an illustration or two drawn on overhead projector slides.

APPROXIMATE TIME REQUIRED: 5 minutes.

SOURCE: Unknown.

I'VE GOT A SECRET

OBJECTIVE: To afford individual introductions in a fun way.

PROCEDURE: At the beginning of a seminar, or at a luncheon or dinner session, comment on the importance of informality and getting acquainted with other participants. But rather than have individuals introduce themselves, tell the group they will introduce the person to their right. They will have a minute to learn that person's name and organization. Then humorously suggest they divulge some deep, dark secret about themselves that "nobody in the whole wide world knows about them!"

Start the process with the first person who introduces the individual on his/her right. To start things off, the facilitator could begin. Keep things moving quickly and lightly.

If participants are seated at round tables, randomly select any participant. If theater style or U-shape seating is used, start introductions in the front of room. (NOTE: This method is usable with groups of up to 50 people. It may be overly time consuming for larger groups.)

MATERIALS
REQUIRED: None.

APPROXIMATE
TIME REQUIRED: 10-15 minutes depending on size of group.

SOURCE: Unknown.

MERRY BIRTHDAY?/HAPPY CHRISTMAS?

OBJECTIVE: To provide a sure-fire way to match up workshop participants for mutual introductions or any other two-person activity.

PROCEDURE: Collect a set of used greeting cards you have received. Examples include birthday, Christmas, Easter, Thanksgiving, anniversary, first communion/confirmation card etc.

Cut off all but the first page.

Cut the first page in half. You may wish to strategically cut the page in two, dividing the major greeting into two parts (such as "Happy" and "Anniversary"). This will provide a slightly greater challenge for participants, who then cannot just call out for a "Birthday" partner, but must match the entire message.

Distribute one-half of a card to each participant, making sure that both halves of each card are distributed within the group. This may necessitate waiting until all participants have appeared (if you historically have no-shows in your groups). You may also need to warn them that they must not only get the major greeting correct (e.g., "Happy Birthday") but also the verse on the card.

Instruct them to mix with each other until they find the person holding the other half of the card. Then they should uncover enough interesting information about that person to enable them to effectively introduce that person to the rest of the group when you give the signal.

Note: You may also wish to point out to the participants that this is effectively a group task, since if any two people get the wrong match ("Happy Christmas"), then two others will also be stuck with the wrong match ("Merry Birthday").

MATERIALS REQUIRED: Several dozen used greeting cards.

APPROXIMATE TIME REQUIRED: About 15 minutes for distribution and discovery of partners, plus adequate time for mutual introductions, depending on the size of the group.

SOURCE: John Newstrom, Duluth, MN.

YOU OUGHT TO BE IN PICTURES

OBJECTIVE: To be used as a get-acquainted exercise in large groups (over 100).

PROCEDURE: As people enter the room, each is given a 3 x 5 preprinted card or sheet as shown on the page 33. Participants are asked to circulate around the room and seek out 2-3 additional characters from that TV series or movie. As soon as the card is properly completed, the winning groups are called forward for token door prizes. (NOTE: The character for each person's card is filled in prior to being given the form, i.e., Your character is: "WIZARD OF OZ".

**MATERIALS
REQUIRED:**   One 3 x 5 card or sheet for each attendee. (See page 33 for sample format.)

**APPROXIMATE
TIME REQUIRED:** 15-20 minutes.

SOURCE: ASTD National Membership Management Task Force.

WELCOME

Your task is to find at least two (2) other participants with whom your character stars in either a movie, cartoon, or TV series:

Your character is: _____

Your co-stars are:

CHARACTER	NAME
_____	_____
_____	_____
_____	_____

Other characters can be taken from current films, television programs or even the organization itself.

THE WALKING BILLBOARD

OBJECTIVE: To provide a novel way to stimulate participants to mingle and share key information with each other.

PROCEDURE: Tell the group that they have the opportunity to design their own get-acquainted session. Ask them to propose major factors that they would like to discover about other participants in the session. List these for them all to see. Examples might include:

a. favorite food
b. pet peeve
c. best book recently read
d. all-time favorite movie (or actress or actor)
e. ideal vacation

Ask for a quick show of hands regarding the three most useful items from the items generated. Using a rough tabulation, select the five or six items receiving the greatest support, and identify those for the group.

Provide every participant with a sheet of flip chart paper and a marker. Ask them to place their name at the top, and then list the 5-6 categories down the left side, and answer each for themselves.

Now (and this will produce some laughter) use masking tape to attach the sheet to the person's shoulders (they will look like a walking billboard). Then invite them all to walk around the room and discover who everyone is. (Further exploration of what is written is encouraged.)

DISCUSSION QUESTIONS: What are your reactions to this group-designed method of ice-breaking?

Now that we've done it once, what new categories of information would you like to seek (and share!) if we were to repeat it later in the program?

MATERIALS REQUIRED: Flip chart paper and a marker for each participant; masking tape.

APPROXIMATE TIME REQUIRED: 15-20 minutes (you may have to put a stop to the mingling!).

SOURCE: Mary DeVine, Phoenix, AZ.

MIDDLE NAME GAME

OBJECTIVE: To be used as an initial icebreaker for groups of 25 or less.

PROCEDURE: Each participant is asked to give his/her middle name and tell how or why that particular name was chosen. The trainer should begin the process, and if appropriate, do so in a light, humorous way.

**MATERIALS
REQUIRED:** None.

**APPROXIMATE
TIME REQUIRED:** 10-15 minutes.

SOURCE: Unknown.

SELF-DISCLOSURE INTRODUCTIONS

OBJECTIVE: To provide innovative ways of introducing members to each other.

PROCEDURES: Instruct participants to take two items (e.g., family pictures, credit cards, rabbits' feet) from their purses, wallets, or pockets. When introducing themselves to the group, they should then use whatever they took out to help describe themselves in at least two ways (e.g., "I am superstitious"; "I'm such a tightwad that this is the first dollar I ever earned").

Ask each participant to state his/her name and attach an adjective that not only describes a dominant characteristic, but also starts with the first letter of her/his name (e.g., Sensuous Stan, Marvelous Mary, Inscrutable Ida, Dancing Diane, etc.).

Group members introduce themselves by name but also provide a nickname that they now have, once had, or would be willing to have if they could pick their own. Then, during breaks, members are encouraged to circulate and explore the reasons behind the announced nicknames.

Before introductions begin, ask the group members to brainstorm a list of provocative questions they would like to have each other answer (and be willing to do so). Have them screen the list to throw out those in questionable taste, and select the 2-3 that everyone feels comfortable with. Proceeed with introductions that incorporate answers to the questions.

Distribute 3 x 5 cards containing participants' names, and a small number of items to be filled in on separate lines. When participants complete the items, have them pin, tape, or hold the cards up in front of them as they circulate in the room, allowing others to engage them in exploratory conversations about the items. Sample questions include: "The person living today whom I most admire is _____"; "My favorite all-time vacation was spent at _____"; "The best book/movie I ever read/saw was _____."

**APPROXIMATE
TIME REQUIRED:** One minute per person.

**MATERIALS
REQUIRED:**   None.

SOURCES: Varied.

39

THROW AWAY YOUR TROUBLES

OBJECTIVE: To enable participants to get several responses to an individual problem or concern.

PROCEDURE: This exercise can be used at almost any time during a training session. For programs over a half-day in length, this activity can be used intermittently during the course. Announce that participants will now have a chance to "throw away" their problems. Have each person think of a question, problem, or concern about the topic being addressed. (If s/he cannot think of a relevant item, any problem is OK). After participants write out their anonymous particular problems ask them to crumple up the paper and throw it in a container (a box or receptacle that will be placed in the center of the room). For larger groups, have several containers around the room. Be sure not to use regular waste baskets unless they are empty!

After all papers are in the receptacles, ask any person to pick out a crumpled paper and toss it to anyone in the room. Whoever catches it opens the paper and reads the problem aloud. A 3-person team is formed (one on each side of the "receiver"). The team is given a "30-second timeout" to discuss possible solutions or answers. During this time, the rest of the group is asked to jot down 2-3 answers or responses.

The team gives its responses followed by others in the group who can assist.

Repeat the process as time permits.

MATERIALS REQUIRED: Paper, pencils, empty boxes or containers.

APPROXIMATE TIME REQUIRED: Minimum four-five minutes; expanded as time available.

SOURCE: Unknown.

TREASURE HUNT

OBJECTIVE: To be used for small-group (15-25 attendees) workshops as a get-acquainted activity.

PROCEDURE: At the very start of the seminar, explain the importance of becoming acquainted with the other participants. Hand out a form (see page 45) to to each attendee and ask that everyone find at least one similarity (e.g., "grew up in Chicago") and one dissimilar trait (e.g., "football fanatic" vs. "dislike sports") for at least 8-10 other participants. Award a small prize for the first person completing the form.

MATERIALS REQUIRED: Handout forms and nominal prize.

APPROXIMATE TIME REQUIRED: 15-20 minutes.

SOURCE: Gordon Hills, St. Petersburg, FL.

TREASURE HUNT

INSTRUCTIONS: Write your name on the first line. Circulate around the room finding one trait you have in common (i.e., "newcomer to city") and one item quite dissimilar (i.e., "has worked for same organization over 10 years" vs. "third job this year!")

	NAME	ALIKE	DIFFERENT
1.	_____	_____	_____
2.	_____	_____	_____
3.	_____	_____	_____
4.	_____	_____	_____
5.	_____	_____	_____
6.	_____	_____	_____
7.	_____	_____	_____
8.	_____	_____	_____
9.	_____	_____	_____
10.	_____	_____	_____

II.

LEARNING

BINGO REVIEW

OBJECTIVE: To assess the degree of retention of key concepts among a group of trainees.

To reinforce major terms at the end of a training session.

PROCEDURE: Develop a set of 24-25 questions about the subject material that can each be answered with a standard term from the training program.

Sort them into five major categories. Create some identity of each category name with the letters, B, I, N, G, and O.

Create BINGO cards for each participant. Two options exist.

a.   Generic cards. These would be exactly like traditional BINGO cards, with numbers in each of the 24 cells in the 5 x 5 matrix (the middle cell is "Free." In this scenario, the trainer would read a question with an associated number, and if the trainee had the number and could correctly write in the answer, (s)he could fill in the cell.

b.   Specific cards. These would have the cells previously filled in with 24 of the key terms (plus a "free" one in the middle). Whenever a question is read, if the participant believes that one of the answers on the card fits the question, (s)he could simply write in the question number next to it.

Whenever a participant achieves five correct answers in a row (either vertically, horizontally, or diagonally), (s)he may call out "BINGO" and receive a prize. Play may continue until all 25 cells are filled, too.

DISCUSSION QUESTIONS: Which terms gave the group the greatest difficulty?

Which terms would you now like to have clarified?

MATERIALS REQUIRED: A set of questions, plus a card for each participant. Inexpensive prizes.

APPROXIMATE
TIME REQUIRED: 15-30 minutes, depending on degree of explanation of terms required upon completion of the game.

SOURCE: Gerry Reid, IT Services.

BINGO GAME BOARD

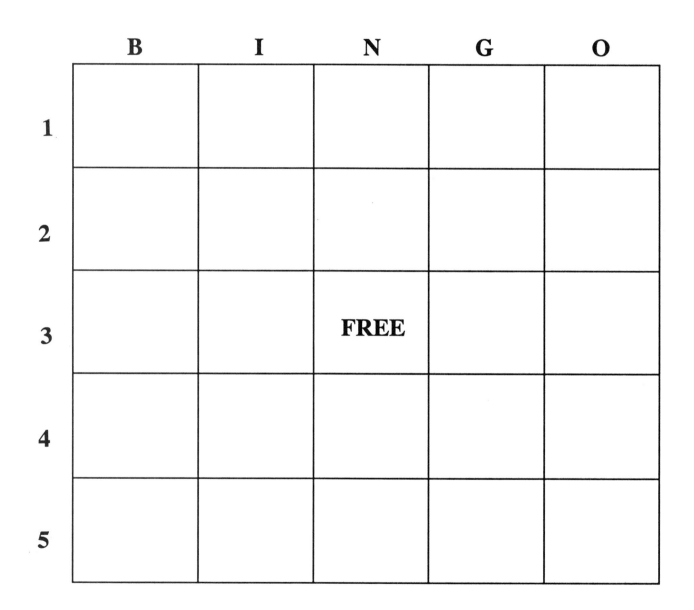

BUT I'VE ALWAYS DONE IT THAT WAY...

OBJECTIVE: To illustrate how easy it is to develop and continue using unconscious habits.

To point out that there are often equally effective alternative ways to accomplish an objective.

To illustrate that old ways of doing things may interfere with our acquisition of new behaviors, and therefore require "unlearning" first.

PROCEDURE: Ask one or more participants (e.g., all those wearing a suit coat, sports jacket, or even a windbreaker or cardigan sweater) to stand and remove their coats.

Ask them to put the coats on, noting which arm went in first.

Ask them to take the coats off again, and put them on this time by putting the other arm in first.

DISCUSSION QUESTIONS: How did it feel to reverse your normal pattern of donning your jacket? (How did it look to observers who were watching?)

Why was it so tough (awkward) to do?

What prevents us from adopting new ways to doing things? How can we make changes without old habits interfering with them?

How can we open ourselves to change within the program, and accept the fact that there may be equally effective (or better) ways to accomplish our tasks then we've used before?

MATERIALS REQUIRED: None.

APPROXIMATE TIME REQUIRED: Five-ten minutes.

SOURCE: Bob Holmes, Mt. Olive, AL.

COME ON OVER

OBJECTIVE: To use just before break; to demonstrate that nonresistance may actually work in your favor.

PROCEDURE: Ask attendees to stand, pairoff and face each other. Designate one person as "A," the second as "B." Partners place their hands against each other with palms open and forward. Ask each group to push hands against the other with firm pressure. Tell "A" partners to "give in" (i.e., stop pushing forward) anytime without warning "B." Reverse roles and repeat exercise.

DISCUSSION
QUESTIONS: How did it feel when the other person quit resisting?

How did it feel when you exerted continued pressure when there was no resistance (seemed foolish, "pressure" wasn't necessary, etc.)?

"Pushing" or unnecessary strength or pressure can sometimes be counterproductive. Can you think of some examples when this has happened?

MATERIALS
REQUIRED: None.

APPROXIMATE
TIME REQUIRED: Three-four minutes.

SOURCE: Carol Klein-Zemp, Arizona Heart Institute, Phoenix, AZ.

MATCHING REVIEW

OBJECTIVE: To assess the degree of retention of key concepts among a group of trainees.

To reinforce major terms at the end of a training session (or module).

PROCEDURE: Develop a master set of key vocabulary terms associated with the training program.

Create a master list of the definitions of each term on one set of pages, and a numbered list of the actual terms on another set of pages. (The terms, of course, should be in scrambled order--different from definitions.)

Divide the group into teams of 2-5 persons, and give each team a set of materials to work with.

Set a time limit for the exercise. Score each group on the number of correctly matched terms they identify as a group within the time period allotted to them. Provide prizes to the winning team. Then proceed to clarify the more difficult terms.

DISCUSSION QUESTIONS: Which terms gave the group the greatest difficulty? Why?

Which terms would you now like to have clarified?

MATERIALS REQUIRED: Previously prepared matching exercises, one set for each team. Inexpensive prizes.

APPROXIMATE TIME REQUIRED: Totally dependent on the number of terms, and familiarity of the players with the terms.

SOURCE: Unknown.

"NEW DIRECTIONS" IN LEARNING

OBJECTIVES: To demonstrate to the group that prior learning (knowledge, skills, and attitudes) has a powerful and often negative effect on their capacity and willingness to adopt new learning.

To explore ways to facilitate the "unlearning" process.

PROCEDURE: Present the group with a handout or visual display showing the new directions you would like to have them learn (see page 61).

Give them several minutes to absorb the connection between the "old" way and the "new" way.

When all are ready, have them set aside their handouts and stand up, facing the front of the room. Test them on their "new directions" by calling out the old directions and seeing how many of them successfully point in the new directions. (Note: If you wish to confound them further, line them up in two rows facing each other!) Give them ten commands, and ask them to keep score of their accuracy.

What can you do to help your trainees unlearn the old, thus better preparing them to learn the new?

MATERIALS REQUIRED: The handout or visual showing the old and the new directions (see page 61).

APPROXIMATE TIME REQUIRED: 10 minutes, plus discussion time.

SOURCE: See John W. Newstrom, "The Management of Unlearning: Exploding the "Clean Slate" Fallacy," Training and Development Journal, August 1983, pp. 36-39.

NEW DIRECTIONS TO LEARNING

OLD DIRECTIONS	NEW DIRECTIONS
UP	RIGHT
DOWN	REAR
LEFT	DOWN
RIGHT	FRONT
FRONT	UP
REAR	LEFT

STOP THE MUSIC!

OBJECTIVE: To energize a group after lunch.

To enable participants to relax and to get acquainted.

PROCEDURE: Prepare questions (one short question on each card) about the organization or topic being taught.

Set up the meeting room in your favorite style, with extra space around each chair. (When starting the exercise, remove all extra chairs and one more.)

Describe the activity to participants. Have the participants walk around the room while you play up-beat music. After 20-30 seconds, stop the music. The participants should now all scramble for chairs. The lucky person left standing gets a card to answer.

Remove one chair and continue playing for 4-5 more turns.

MATERIALS REQUIRED: Question cards, music.

APPROXIMATE TIME REQUIRED: 10-20 minutes maximum. Exercise may be stopped at any time. Don't spend too much time, as its main purpose is for energizing group.

COMMENT: After the exercise, give prizes (tapes, candy, handouts, etc.) to those who answered questions, with the comment that often the person who looks like a loser is the winner in the long run.

SOURCE: Ginger G. Derekson, Unlimited Futures Consulting, Owensboro, KY.

PREVIEW/REVIEW

OBJECTIVE: To introduce new terms/key terms to a training group before the actual training begins, thus clueing them as to what the most important (or unique) terms and concepts will be (preview).

To provide a refreshing format for reiterating the most critical concepts and cementing them in the participants' minds, while avoiding the classically boring "Now to summarize for you..."

PROCEDURE: Study the entire content to be covered within a training course or module of it. Select several dozen of the most critical concepts or terms, and write each one and its brief definition on 3 x 5 cards.

Form the workshop participants into several small groups (e.g., five persons each). Distribute blank cards to each team member.

Select one team and one term. Ask all team members to write the definition of each term on their first card.

Collect the cards and mix in the correct-definition card with the others. Read each definition to the other teams, and ask them to individually designate which definition they think is most correct (a response sheet may be used to record their answers).

Move to the second team, and second term. Continue until all terms have been covered. Tabulate the number of correct answers within each team, and announce the "winner." (Ideally, some prize of nominal value will be awarded to its members.)

Note: This game may be used effectively at either the beginning or end of a training session for preview or review purposes.

DISCUSSION QUESTIONS: Which of the terms still requires some additional explanation?

How was this exercise useful to you in solidifying your ability to recall key terms from the course?

MATERIALS REQUIRED: List of key terms; 3 x 5 cards; response sheets (multiple choice).

APPROXIMATE TIME REQUIRED: 15-20 Minutes.

SOURCE: Unknown.

THE NO-TEST TEST

OBJECTIVE: To enable participants to summarize the content covered in the seminar.

PROCEDURE: Approximately 30 minutes prior to the end of the half- (or full-) day seminar, subdivide participants into groups of 3-4. Their task is to first identify the 3-4 most important points they learned and to brainstorm a way to help them remember them. Depending on time, ask a few groups to report their findings.

MATERIALS REQUIRED: None.

APPROXIMATE TIME REQUIRED: 15-20 minutes.

SOURCE: Unknown.

RESISTANCE TO CHANGE

OBJECTIVE: To demonstrate to participants that they need to confront their own resistance to change before they can achieve the greatest benefit from the current training experience.

PROCEDURE: Tell the group to assume that you have developed a new product that has tremendous potential organizational benefits. (A good example is the Dvorak Simplified Keyboard for typewriters and word processors, which allegedly had potential to increase operator efficiency by over 40%; see illustration on page 71.)

Ask the group to list all the positive reasons why people should discontinue using the old "QWERTY" keyboards and adapt the new Dvorak system.

Now ask the group to predict all the reasons why people will resist using the new keyboard. Then ask them to categorize those reasons as primarily rational (e.g., too costly, too bulky, wrong size) or primarily emotional (e.g., "I'd have to learn something new").

Now tell them that you plan to introduce them to some new ideas in this training program that have the potential to improve their personal and organizational effectiveness.

a.   Ask them to predict why they and others will resist embracing the new ideas/methods. Which of these factors are rational, and which are emotional?

b.   Ask them to list the positive reasons why they should be open to the new ideas/methods you will discuss.

DISCUSSION QUESTIONS: Why do we tend to think that other people (but not us) resist change?

What can we do to better facilitate change in other people?

What can I do in this program to make it more likely that you will accept that changes I offer to you?

What will you commit yourselves to do to make yourself more open to the changes you will hear about?

MATERIALS
REQUIRED: Overhead transparency of Dvorak keyboard, if desired.

APPROXIMATE
TIME REQUIRED: 15-20 minutes.

SOURCE: Adapted from Tom Reilly, Ellisville, MO.

DVORAK SIMPLIFIED KEYBOARD

7	5	3	1	9	0	2	4	6	8	+ =
: ?	' "	. ,	P	Y	F	G	C	R	L	& /
A	O	E	U	I	D	H	T	N	S	- _
; :	Q	J	K	X	B	M	W	V	Z

22%

70%

8%

Shift

Shift

space bar

WHO CARES?

OBJECTIVE: To allow individuals to identify a quality about themselves and to translate that trait into a benefit.

PROCEDURE: Toss a foam ball randomly into the audience. The person who catches the ball stands up, gives her/his name and states a quality about her/himself, a product s/he sells or distributes, or anything else about her/himself or organization. The audience responds "Who cares?" The individual then translates the stated fact or quality into a benefit or an advantage, or states what the item means to the client or customer. The individual then throws the ball to someone else. Repeat the procedure as time allows.

**MATERIALS
REQUIRED:** Foam Nerfball (or simply a lightweight object).

**APPROXIMATE
TIME REQUIRED:** 15-20 minutes.

SOURCE: Pam Lontos, Thousand Oaks, CA.

TALE OF THE PROCESSIONARY CATERPILLARS

OBJECTIVE: To stimulate trainees to be aware of the dangers of passively accepting what others say and do.

PROCEDURE: Share this tale with the group: There is a type of caterpillar called a processionary caterpillar, so named because one will establish a direction and all the others will fall in very closely behind and move in the same path. As a matter of fact, the followers' behavior becomes so automatic that their eyes become half-closed as they shut out the world around them and let the leader do all the thinking and decision making about which direction to pursue. Their behavior is rote and automatic.

An experiment by the French naturalist Jean-Henri Fabre demonstrated the rigidity of the processionary caterpillars' behavior when he enticed the leader to start circling the edge of a large flower pot. The other caterpillars followed suit in a tight procession, forming a closed circle in which the distinctions between leader and follower became totally blurred, and the path had no beginning and no ending. Instead of soon getting bored with the nonproductive activity, the caterpillars kept up their mindless search for several days and nights until they dropped off the edge through exhaustion and starvation from lack of food. Relying totally on instinct, past experience, custom, and tradition, the caterpillars achieved nothing because they mistook activity for achievement.

DISCUSSION QUESTIONS: In what ways are employees like processionary caterpillars?

Are trainees like yourselves susceptible of falling prey to the phenomenon of processionary caterpillars? Explain.

How can we prevent ourselves and others from becoming like the caterpillars in this story?

MATERIALS REQUIRED: None.

APPROXIMATE TIME REQUIRED: Five minutes.

SOURCE: H. Kent Baker and Ronald H. Gorman, Washington, DC.

THE COMPANY STORE CATALOG

OBJECTIVE: To encourage active oral participation (depth and/or breadth).

PROCEDURE: Obtain or create some form of distributable currency, such as play money from a "Monopoly" game or a set of poker chips (be sure to establish the relative values of red, white, blue, and yellow chips in advance).

Create a "Company Store Catalog" by accumulating a number of potentially valued prizes for the training session participants. These might include gift certificates from the company cafeteria worth anywhere from a free cup of coffee to free lunch; a coffee mug with the company logo; a free book relevant to the training course (e.g., <u>What Every Superior Should Know</u>, by Lester Bittel and John Newstrom, or <u>Supervisory Communication</u> by Edward E. Scannell); or more imaginative items such as lunch with the CEO in the executive cafeteria; or two free theater tickets; or a free round of golf. Be imaginative!

Inform trainees of your participative expectations, and the array of rewards available. Then begin rewarding the appropriate behaviors by promptly distributing dollars or chips when the trainees' actions deserve it.

Later, when basic patterns are established, you can further shape desired behaviors by increasing the size of reward offered or making a group reward (e.g., dollars for everyone) contingent upon a specific behavior (e.g., analytical vs. regurgitative responses).

At the end of the training session, allow trainees a few minutes to browse through your "Company Store Catalog" and "buy" the items of their choice.

DISCUSSION QUESTIONS: To what degree did the offer of "rewards" effect your willingness to participate?

Did the reward system distract you in any way? To what degree did it contribute to your learning or retention?

MATERIALS REQUIRED: Play money, chips, or some other suitable form of currency; an array of catalog items.

APPROXIMATE
TIME REQUIRED: Five minutes to explain; 10-15 minutes at the end to sell items.

SOURCE: John Newstrom, Duluth, MN.

HELP WANTED

OBJECTIVE: To measure behavior for a specific job in order to obtain the most suitable applicant. Trainers can make use of this exercise to teach the group interview skills.

PROCEDURE: Groups of four to seven select a job position from a group of want ads that their particular group would agree to apply for. If all members are from different professional areas, then a different position should be selected by the group so that no member has an advantage.

Each group member should then draft a few qualifications, either realistically or hypothetically depending on the position, i.e., a very brief vitae.

A group of three to five individuals should then review the vitae and formulate a few specific questions.

The interview takes place (role play). Interviewers should try to measure the listening ability of the applicants by referring to statements made during the interview at different points. Interviewers should try not to ask each member to respond to all questions and should try not to ask each member to respond to all questions and should not encourage participants to go in order of succession in answering. Leadership should occur and be a measurable behavior.

Interviewers can select the applicant, and they can also select who they think should receive the position.

MATERIALS REQUIRED: Local newspaper want ads.

APPROXIMATE TIME REQUIRED: 25-30 minutes.

SOURCE: Linda McCay, TRI-C Consultants, Scottsdale, AZ.

III.

BRAINTEASERS

IF LIARS CAN FIGURE, CAN FIGURES LIE?

OBJECTIVE: To alert trainees to the fact that they must always be alert to the possibility that what they hear may need to be questioned, examined, and challenged. In other words, their minds must be "in gear" the entire time they are in the training session.

PROCEDURE: Distribute copies of the "quiz" on page 85 to the trainees (alternatively, project a copy of it on an overhead transparency projector).

Create a sense of urgency by indicating that you will only allow exactly two minutes for completion of the test. Ask participants not to disclose their choices until all trainees have finished the test.

Ask the group for their responses (preferably, tabulate the number who underlined each of the seven problems on the chalkboard or on a prepared transparency).

Then, when someone objects that there are only two items arithmetically incorrect (numbers 2 and 3 are false), point out that therefore the initial assertion is false. Consequently, that assertion becomes the third false statement that they were to identify.

DISCUSSION QUESTIONS: Were the directions clear and unambiguous? If so, why were they misinterpreted?

What are the reasons why trainers' statements and assertions are often readily accepted, and almost naively believed?

Under what conditions should trainers' assertions be less-readily accepted and even challenged?

MATERIALS REQUIRED: Copies of "A Simple Arithmetic Test."

APPROXIMATE TIME REQUIRED: Five-ten minutes.

SOURCE: Adapted from Martin Gardner, <u>Aha Gotcha!</u>, San Francisco: W. H. Freeman & Co., 1982, p. 8.

A SIMPLE ARITHMETIC TEST

There are three false statements here. Identify them by underlining each one. Please work quickly. Raise your hand when you are done.

1. $\sqrt{169} = 13$

2. $243 \div 3 = 61$

3. $4 \times 27 = 98$

4. $(213 - 23)/2 = 95$

5. $(7)^3 = 343$

6. $242 - 12/3 = 238$

7. $6^2 + 8^2 = \sqrt{10,000}$

SCRAMBLED CITIES

OBJECTIVE: To be used primarily as an icebreaker.

PROCEDURE: Distribute copies of page 89 to each participant. Each item can be unscrambled to identify a city. Award an inexpensive prize to the first person who completes the quiz correctly. (The answers are given on page 91.)

MATERIALS
REQUIRED: Copies of page 89.

APPROXIMATE
TIME REQUIRED: Five minutes.

SOURCE: Unknown.

SCRAMBLED CITIES

1. OIAPER   _____

2. REEDVN   _____

3. ITSUAN   _____

4. TEEATSL   _____

5. LE OASP   _____

6. LUULOONH   _____

7. WNE ALROESN   _____

8. SNA TANNOOI   _____

9. AKNSSA ITCY   _____

10. SOL SEELGNA   _____

11. SNA SEJO   _____

12. ULBOCKB   _____

13. ACHIWTI   _____

14. XNOIEPH   _____

15. AAPTM   _____

16. ULTAS   _____

17. GACOHIC   _____

18. NAS GOIDE   _____

19. THOUSNO   _____

20. PROTLDAN   _____

ANSWERS

1. Peoria
2. Denver
3. Austin
4. Seattle
5. El Paso
6. Honolulu
7. New Orleans
8. San Antonio
9. Kansas City
10. Los Angeles
11. San Jose
12. Lubbock
13. Wichita
14. Phoenix
15. Tampa
16. Tulsa
17. Chicago
18. San Diego
19. Houston
20. Portland

BRAINTEASERS
(I.Q. Tests)

OBJECTIVE: To be used to introduce any session on creativity, problem-solving, or related topic.

To be used as a "just for fun" or a "change of pace" activity.

PROCEDURE: Hand out copies of any of the following "IQ Tests" (page 95-133, with answers). Suggest that each block represents a well-known phrase or saying.

MATERIALS REQUIRED: Handout sheets for each person or small group.

APPROXIMATE TIME REQUIRED: 5-10 minutes.

SOURCE: Varied.

I.Q. TEST

Here are some real puzzlers for you! Decipher the
hidden meaning of each set of words.

---

1 I FGH JKLMNOP Q RST	2 EILNPU	3 **PLASMA** **H$_2$O**	4 $_M^{O~~N}_{O~~S~~^I~^T}_E$
5 **NOXQQIVIT**	6 **arrest** **you're**	7 RUINS RUINS RUINS RUINS RUINS LOVE RUINS RUINS RUINS	8 **PICT RES**
9 L NCH L NCH	10 44444	11 *DISTANCE*	12 P **NOANO** Y
13 cy cy	14 **B ILL ED**	15 **POLMOMICE**	16 HIGH CLOUDS CLOUDS CLOUDS CLOUDS CLOUDS

95

ANSWERS

1. High IQ
2. Line up
3. Blood is thicker than water
4. Mixed emotions
5. No excuse for it
6. You're under arrest
7. Love among the ruins
8. You ought to be in pictures
9. Take you out to lunch
10. Petifores
11. Distance running
12. Pay through the nose
13. Cyclones
14. Sick in bed
15. Mother-in-law
16. High above the clouds

I.Q. TEST

Here are some real puzzlers for you! Decipher the
hidden meaning of each set of words.

---

1 U S T I	**2** **STROKES!** *STROKES* STROKES	**3** SOM_{ETHING}	**4** **KJUSTK**
5 S T I N K	**6** W A L K G N I K	**7** you just me	**8** M M A P
9 **FISHING** c	**10** GET IT GET IT GET IT GET IT	**11** *more it it thani*	**12** VAD ERS
13 **i.e.** ●	**14** **GOLDEN GATE** H$_2$O	**15** WAY —— PASS	**16** **END** **N** **D**

99

ANSWERS

1. It's up to you
2. Different Strokes
3. The start of something big
4. Just in case
5. Fouled up
6. Jay walking
7. Just between you and me
8. Time's up
9. Deep sea fishing
10. Forget it
11. More to it than meets the eye
12. Space invaders
13. That is beside the point
14. Water under the bridge
15. Highway overpass
16. Making ends meet

102

I.Q. TEST

Here are some real puzzlers for you! Decipher the
hidden meaning of each set of words.

1 **HAMLET WORDS**	**2** d o o d l e	**3** late n e v er	**4** **c l o u**
5 lo head heels ve	**6** THAT	**7** **BED FA ST**	**8** ◯ **ME**
9 **CAR JACK TON**	**10** 1. GLANCE 2. 3. GLANCE	**11** **momanon**	**12** ca se case
13 BEERVODKASH... GINBEERVODKA... RUMGIN...SHERRY	**14** NINTH	**15** c c c c **HOLIDAY**	**16** **S K I I N G**

ANSWERS

1. Play on words
2. Dipsy doodle
3. Better late than never
4. Partly cloudy
5. Head over heels in love
6. Fancy that
7. Bed and breakfast
8. This round is on me
9. Jack-in-the-box
10. Without a second glance
11. Man in the moon
12. Open-and-shut case
13. A round of drinks
14. Middle of the ninth
15. Overseas holiday
16. Downhill skiing

I.Q. TEST

Here are some real puzzlers for you! Decipher the
hidden meaning of each set of words.

---

1 cry m i l k	**2** **MAN** **campus**	**3** 111111 another another another another another another	**4** **BUSINES**
5 C A N C E L L E D	**6**	**7** R O A D	**8** sitting world
9 ME ME ME day AL AL AL	**10** VIT _ MIN	**11** S T E P P I N G	**12** **REVIRDTAES**
13 <u>NO NO</u> CORRECT	**14** head ache	**15** heatheatheatheat	**16** M OUNTAIN

ANSWERS

1. Cry over spilled milk
2. Big man on campus
3. Six of one; half dozen of another
4. Unfinished business
5. Cancelled check
6. Moving in the right circles
7. Middle of the road
8. Sitting on top of the world
9. Three square meals a day
10. Vitamin "A" deficiency
11. Stepping over
12. Backseat driver
13. Right under your nose
14. Splitting headache
15. Heatwave
16. Mountain climbing

I.Q. TEST

Here are some real puzzlers for you! Decipher the
hidden meaning of each set of words.

1 i n w a i t	2 ho ho + ho	3 LOVE SIGHT SIGHT SIGHT	4 **WR*it* ING**
5 G R N E I A N S O	6 N O S^E	7 **PETS A**	8 S O L DANUBE
9 Symphon	10 **encounters** **encounters** **encounters**	11 3. O 2. U 1. T	12 1 3 5 7 9 11 vs. U
13 **eyebrows**	14 r o **rail** d	15 **T RN**	16 budget ∧

ANSWERS

1. Lying in wait
2. Tally ho
3. Love at first sight
4. Put it in writing
5. Circular reasoning
6. Broken nose
7. A step backward
8. Sold down the river
9. Unfinished symphony
10. Close encounters
11. Out numbered 3 to 1
12. Odds are aginst you
13. Raised eyebrows
14. Railroad crossing
15. No U Turn
16. Balanced budget

I.Q. TEST

Here are some real puzzlers for you! Decipher the
hidden meaning of each set of words.

1	2	3	4

belt
hitting
	EXIT
	LEG
		often
		    not
		often
		    not
		often
			night fly

5	6	7	8

MIGR**A**INE	SPRIN**G**
	SUMM**E**R
	AUTUM**N**
	WIN**T**ER
		9ALL5	*once*
			upon
			a
			time N
			        + E
			        S

9	10	11	12
GIVE GET GIVE GET GIVE GET GIVE GET	**breth**	ACC–DENT	**esroh riding**
13	14	15	16
EMPLOY T MEN	wire just	GRIMY SMUDGED FILTHY BESMIRCHED UNWASHED FOUL SOILED TARNISHED UNCLEAN SOOTY SULLIED DUSTY	**DO12"OR**

ANSWERS

1. Hitting below the belt
2. Out on a limb
3. More often then not
4. Fly by night
5. A splitting headache
6. A man for all seasons
7. All in a day's work
8. Westside story
9. Forgive and forget
10. Short of breath
11. Accident prone
12. Horseback riding
13. Men out of work
14. Just under the wire
15. Dirty dozen
16. A foot in the door

I.Q. TEST

Here are some real puzzlers for you! Decipher the
hidden meaning of each set of words.

1 PERSON PERSONS PERSONS PERSONS	2 insult + injury	3 EVARELTO	4 $(S T E A K)^3$
5 NO WAYS IT WAYS	6 ALL world	7 $\underline{1\ 3\ 5\ 7\ 9}$ WHELMING	8 CCCCCCC
9 gettingitall	10 alai	11 CUS TOM	12 MAUD
13 $\frac{\begin{array}{c}T\\T\\+T\end{array}}{3T}$	14 RASINGINGIN	15 FAIRY WOLF DUCKLING	16 24 Hours

ANSWERS

1. First person singular
2. Add insult to injury
3. Elevator out of order
4. Cubed steak
5. No two ways about it
6. It's a small world after all
7. The odds are overwhelming
8. High seas
9. Getting it all together
10. Jai alai
11. A break in custom
12. Mad about you
13. Teetotaler
14. Singing in the rain
15. The good, the bad, the ugly
16. Call it a day

I.Q. TEST

Here are some real puzzlers for you! Decipher the
hidden meaning of each set of words.

1 safe ˢ ʳ ʸ ₒ ʳ	**2** **FUSS** ○	**3** əlddɐəuıd cake	**4** ⌒ TIK ○
5 o **L D**	**6** TILL IME	**7** **J** **O** AN **B**	**8** W O R L
9 P P O D	**10** INITIA _	**11** **FILE**	**12** JUS 144 TICE
13 WOHNICLEE	**14** **L O V**	**15** 1 T 3 4 5 6	**16** **BRING BALLERINAS**

ANSWERS

1. Better safe than sorry
2. Big fuss over nothing
3. Pineapple upside down cake
4. Arctic circle
5. Growing old
6. Till the end of time
7. An inside job
8. World without end
9. Two peas in a pod
10. The first noel
11. Change of life
12. Gross injustice
13. Once in a while
14. Endless love
15. Tea for two
16. Bring on the dancing girls

I.Q. TEST

Here are some real puzzlers for you! Decipher the
hidden meaning of each set of words.

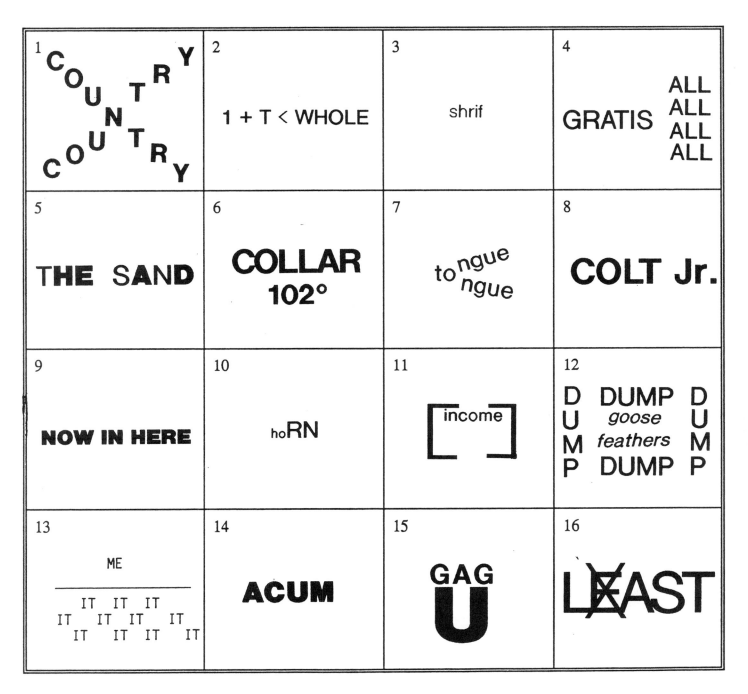

ANSWERS

1. Cross country
2. The whole is greater than the sum of its parts.
3. Short shrift
4. Free for all
5. Head in the sand
6. Hot under the collar
7. Forked tongue or tongue twister
8. Son of a gun
9. Nowhere in sight
10. Little Big Horn
11. High income brackets
12. Down in the dumps
13. It's below me
14. See you in the morning
15. The gag's on you
16. Last but not least

I.Q. TEST

Here are some real puzzlers for you! Decipher the
hidden meaning of each set of words.

1 L E S O D U B **TENNIS**	2 timing tim ing	3 **JJJ BBB**	4 1/4 1/4 1/4 1/4 1/4
5 hand hand hand deck	6 e e q u a i s m c	7 *goodbye*	8 **DR. DR.**
9 dipping	10 fighting	11 S O E S H W R	12 **GGES EGSG** **GEGS SEGG**
13 HEAD SHOULDERS ARMS BODY LEGS ANKLES FEET TOES	14 K A N E L	15 a chance n	16 THE END ↑

ANSWERS

1. Mixed doubles tennis
2. Split second timing
3. The birds and the bees
4. Close quarters
5. All hands on deck
6. $E = MC^2$
7. Waving goodbye
8. A paradox
9. Skinny dipping
10. Two black eyes
11. Scattered showers
12. Scrambled eggs
13. Head and shoulders above the rest
14. Twisted ankle
15. An outside chance
16. Beginning of the end

IV.

PERCEPTION

WHERE YOU STAND DEPENDS ON WHERE YOU SIT

OBJECTIVE: To encourage participants to broaden their horizons, and look upon their environments as opportunities, not as limitations.

PROCEDURE: Present the top half of the figure on page 139 to participants, preferably by projection on a screen so all can see it at once.

Ask how many think that Circle A is larger, and how many think Circle B is larger.

Demonstrate, through revelation of the bottom half of the figure, that both circles are really the same size.

(For a laugh) Ask how many think that Box A is larger, and how many think that Box B is larger. Now you'll really have them worried!

DISCUSSION QUESTIONS: Why does one circle appear larger than the other?

In what ways do we let our minds work in similar fashion as we view our worlds? What impact does this predilection (e.g., to focus on constraints, problems, and barriers) have on our own productivity?

How can we prevent or diminish our tendency to limit our own thinking patterns like this?

Does the apparent truism "Where you stand depends on where you sit" necessarily hold equally true regarding our thought processes and perceptions (e.g., "what we perceive is what we will react to")?

MATERIALS REQUIRED: One transparency, or separate handouts of the top half of the figure for each participant.

APPROXIMATE TIME REQUIRED: Five-ten minutes.

SOURCE: Ryder Systems; Inc., advertisement in <u>Fortune</u>, September 14, 1987.

WHICH CIRCLE APPEARS LARGER?

A   B

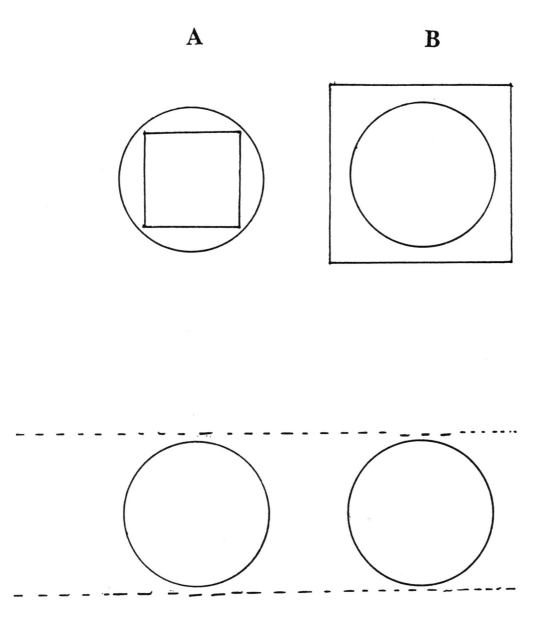

LET'S BE FAIR ABOUT THIS...

OBJECTIVE: To stress the importance of perceptions of equity and fairness in any contact or negotiation between individuals.

PROCEDURE: Identify two participants to role-play an interaction.

Visibly provide Individual **A** with a supply of goods to distribute to (share with) Individual **B**. This may be $100 in (play) money, 100 jelly beans or M & Ms, etc. Instruct Individual **A** that s/he is to make an offer to split the resource with Individual **B** in any proportion desired. Individual **B** may only accept or reject the offer, but not negotiate the split. If **B** accepts the offer, a deal is made. If **B** rejects the offer, neither party receives any of the items.

Inform Individual **B** that **A** has 100 of the resource items to be shared between them. **B** can accept or reject the single offer to be made, but may not provide any input into **A**'s determination of the offer, nor may a counteroffer be made. If **B** rejects the offer, neither party keeps any of the proceeds.

Proceed with the interaction.

KEY: **A** often is tempted to offer a split that will be personally favorable, such as 60-40, or 80-20. From a rational perspective, **B** should accept any offer from **A** since **B** will be better off with <u>anything</u> (even 1) than previously. But since people don't like to be exploited, many **B**'s will reject offers that don't seem <u>fair</u> (as perceived by them). Similarly, **A** could decide to offer any split (even 1-99), since that would make **A** better off than previously. Apparently, the key to making a deal of this kind--even when in a power position--is not only to convince the other party that they will gain a lot over their previous condition, but also to create an image of fairness, wherein **B** is convinced that **A** won't be gaining a lot more than **B**. Negotiators may need to understand that even when it is possible to "make a killing" on a single deal, it may be wiser to build a longer-term relationship by offering a fair deal. This requires, of course, either empathizing sufficiently to infer what is fair, or inquiring of the other party what would be a fair resolution to the situation.

MATERIALS REQUIRED: A substantial supply of a tangible, and mutually desirable item.

APPROXIMATE
TIME REQUIRED: 15 minutes.

SOURCE: Robert H. Frank, Passions Within Reason.

MYTHOLOGIZING (Constructing or Reacting Myths)

OBJECTIVE: To dramatically illustrate to a group that it is easy for them to hold mistaken perceptions about the topic of interest.

PROCEDURE: Define "myth" for them--"a fiction or half-truth that appeals to the consciousness of people while expressing some of their deep, commonly felt emotions."

Progressively disclose to them some common myths in our society today, such as:

a. One size fits all.
b. You're only as old as you feel.
c. The check is in the mail.
d. Money is the root of all evil.
e. I'm from the government, and I'm here to help you.
f. It'll only take a minute to fix this.
g. There's nothing really wrong with you.
h. There is no discrimination in this organization.
i. Everybody is doing it his/her way.

Then add one or more myths pertinent to the topic of the current training session, such as:

a. Once a customer sees our new product, it will sell itself.
b. Our new procedure for doing this is much easier (or simpler, faster, cheaper) than before.

Then proceed to focus on the myth by asking the questions shown below.

DISCUSSION QUESTIONS: Where might this myth have come from?

What factors contribute to its perpetuation?

What can we do to dispel this myth?

It is indeed a myth, or is there a large measure of truth to it?

MATERIALS REQUIRED: None, unless you desire to display the original list visually.

APPROXIMATE
TIME REQUIRED: A few minutes to introduce the myths, and then the myth theme can be woven through the remainder of your presentation.

SOURCE: Unknown.

PORTRAIT OF MY JOB

OBJECTIVE: To get a perception (individually or collectively) of how people "see" their jobs.

PROCEDURE: Break up into groups of 3-4 and ask individuals in each group to draw or sketch out a picture of their jobs or organizations. Pictures can be of TV shows, sports, or anything that describes their perceptions. Groups draw on flip chart paper and describe.

DISCUSSION
QUESTIONS: How do you "see" your job?

How do you fit in?

Has this perception changed recently? How? Why?

How do you think your customers (or colleagues or competition) see your organization?

MATERIALS
REQUIRED: Flip charts.

APPROXIMATE
TIME REQUIRED: 15 minutes.

SOURCE: Renee Howard, Dillards, Tempe, AZ;
Linda McCay, TRI-C Consultants, Scottsdale, AZ.

I'M IMPORTANT, BUT ARE YOU?

OBJECTIVE: To dispel the notion that we automatically know how others feel about themselves.

To serve as a basis for discussion about stereotypes.

To point out that what we think is "common sense" may need to be documented through substantive research.

PROCEDURE: Distribute copies of the "Are You Important?" worksheet (on page 149) to all participants. Have them complete both Part A and B.

Tabulate the responses to Part A. If the group contains both males and females, or blacks and whites, you may choose to sort data by subgroup. It may also help to have a prestructured worksheet for accumulating the data within pages, like the following:

%	# of males	# of females
0-10		
11-20		
21-30		
31-40		
41-50		
51-60		
61-70		
71-80		
81-90		
91-100		

Estimate a mean response for each column. Repeat the process for the three questions in Part B.

Now share this data with the group. "According to normative data collected in the late 1980s from 2,600 individuals of varying socioeconomic backgrounds who lived in seven communities within different regions of the U.S., 49% of white males agreed with the statement, 69% of white females agreed with the statement, and 80% of the black males agreed with the statement."

DISCUSSION
QUESTIONS: How accurate were you individually? Collectively?

How accurate were you individually? Collectively?

What factors led some of you to be less than reasonably accurate? quite accurate? What role do stereotypes play?

What factors contribute to one's feelings of importance?

MATERIALS
REQUIRED: Copies of questionnaire, or an overhead transparency of it.

APPROXIMATE
TIME REQUIRED: Five minutes, plus discussion.

SOURCE: Adapted from <u>Psychology Today</u>, April, 1990.

ARE YOU IMPORTANT?
HOW IMPORTANT ARE OTHERS?

PART A:

Indicate with a check mark whether you agree or disagree with this statement:

"I am an important person."

_____ Agree

_____ Disagree

PART B:

Indicate the percentage (from 0-100%) of each of the following groups that you predict would agree with the statement "I am an important person."

_____ White males

_____ Black males

_____ White females

SUCCESS IS...

OBJECTIVE: To illustrate how values and concepts may change with maturity and experience.

PROCEDURE: In discussion of interpersonal or managerial skills (or any related topic), encourage participants to think about "success." Then ask them to write out or discuss their responses to these questions:

When you were in grade school, how did you define success (i.e., in terms of money, well-known celebrities, etc.)?

When you got out of school (college or high school), how did you define success?

Now--right now--how do you define or identify success?

DISCUSSION QUESTIONS: How many of us--as children--identified success as "making $___,000; becoming a movie star, celebrity, etc.

Did those answers change as you left school? Why or why not?

Why do most of us now look at success so differently? (In all likelihood, most participants will equate success in nonmonetary or nonmaterialistic terms.) Many will identify quality of life, peace of mind, excellent relationships, etc.

MATERIALS REQUIRED: None.

APPROXIMATE TIME REQUIRED: 10-15 minutes.

SOURCE: Unknown.

I WISH, I WISH...

OBJECTIVE: To determine real problem areas of a company.

PROCEDURE: When doing personal interviews with employees, ask if they had a "wish list" and if they could change anything about their job, what would it be? (RESULT: Honest answers.)

DISCUSSION QUESTIONS: What do you like best about your job?

If you were "king/queen for a day", what would you change in the organization (your job, your office, etc.)?

What could we do to make your job better (easier, more fun, etc.)?

What would your boss make as his/her wish?

MATERIALS REQUIRED: None.

APPROXIMATE TIME REQUIRED: 20-30 minutes for interviews.

SOURCE: Heidi Hougham, University of Phoenix, Phoenix, AZ.

MEET YOUR FRIENDLY TRAINER

OBJECTIVE: To make people aware of the importance (or fallacy) of first impressions.

PROCEDURE: At the start of the session after a brief introduction, mention the importance of first impressions and how quickly (3-4 minutes at most) many of us make these first impressions. Suggest that while first impressions may become lasting impressions, initial perception may or may not be accurate. As an example, ask participants to write down 4-5 words that describe you. Do so humorously and explain that any words are fair game. Record the responses on a flip chart, or simply repeat them vocally. Refer back to these lists at the conclusion of the session. Compare the first perceptions to their impressions. Keep the discussion upbeat. Use self-deprecating humor, if necessary.

DISCUSSION QUESTIONS: How many of us tend to make first impressions based on perception?

Were most of these perceptions accurate?

Can you recall an incident when these initial perceptions might have caused problems?

MATERIALS REQUIRED: Flip chart.

APPROXIMATE TIME REQUIRED: Five-ten minutes.

SOURCE: Dr. Nell Jones, Partnerships, Dublin, Ireland
Donald W. H. MacDonald, Auckland, New Zealand.

MANAGING EXPECTATIONS

OBJECTIVE: To alert participants to the ease with which people form first impressions (positive or negative) based on very limited information.

To point out the importance of perception, and the opportunity to manage others' expectations of us contingent on the cues we provide to them.

PROCEDURE: Prepare sufficient copies of the two following forms (pages 159 and 161) to give one to half the group, and the other to the remaining group members.

Distribute the questionnaires to the group without disclosing the differences between them, and collect the forms from them when they are completed.

Tabulate the results for each group. This can be done on an item-by-item basis, or by overall score (to speed up the process). Report the mean results to the group, first alerting them to the fact that the two descriptions differed by only one word (e.g., "cold" vs. "warm").

**DISCUSSION
QUESTIONS:**   To what degree were the evaluations different? Is this reasonable, given the one-word difference between the two biographical descriptions?

What kind of cues do our audiences use to develop overall perceptions of us?

What steps could we take to better manage the perceptions and expectations of our audiences?

**MATERIALS
REQUIRED:**   Two sets of evaluation forms.

**APPROXIMATE
TIME REQUIRED:** 15 minutes, plus tabulation time.

SOURCE: William B. Diggs, Glenside, PA.

ASSESSING THE PROFESSOR

INTRODUCTION: Dr. Nielson is a Professor of Philosophy at a local college. His primary interest is in the relationship and application of philosophical belief systems to a variety of contemporary issues in society. He has taught for over 10 years at two different institutions. He is now 35 years old, married, and has three children and a pet black labrador. His friends describe him as industrious, cold, critical, practical, and determined. He likes to read, take walks, and attend plays.

DIRECTIONS: To the best of your ability, evaluate Dr. Nielson on the following characteristics by circling the appropriate number for each quality. (NOTE: "1" indicates "most descriptive"; "7" idicates "least descriptive").

Knows his stuff	1	2	3	4	5	6	7	Doesn't know his stuff
Considerate of others	1	2	3	4	5	6	7	Self-centered
Modest	1	2	3	4	5	6	7	Proud
Sociable	1	2	3	4	5	6	7	Unsociable
Self-assured	1	2	3	4	5	6	7	Uncertain of himself
Generous	1	2	3	4	5	6	7	Ungenerous
Warm	1	2	3	4	5	6	7	Cold
Humorous	1	2	3	4	5	6	7	Humorless
Important	1	2	3	4	5	6	7	Ruthless

ASSESSING THE PROFESSOR

INTRODUCTION: Dr. Nielson is a Professor of Philosophy at a local college. His primary interest is in the relationship and application of philosophical belief systems to a variety of contemporary issues in society. He has taught for over 10 years at two different institutions. He is now 35 years old, married, and has three children and a pet black labrador. His friends describe him as industrious, warm, critical, practical, and determined. He likes to read, take walks, and attend plays.

DIRECTIONS: To the best of your ability, evaluate Dr. Nielson on the following characteristics by circling the appropriate number for each quality. (NOTE: "1" indicates "most descriptive"; "7" idicates "least descriptive").

Knows his stuff	1	2	3	4	5	6	7	Doesn't know his stuff
Considerate of others	1	2	3	4	5	6	7	Self-centered
Modest	1	2	3	4	5	6	7	Proud
Sociable	1	2	3	4	5	6	7	Unsociable
Self-assured	1	2	3	4	5	6	7	Uncertain of himself
Generous	1	2	3	4	5	6	7	Ungenerous
Warm	1	2	3	4	5	6	7	Cold
Humorous	1	2	3	4	5	6	7	Humorless
Important	1	2	3	4	5	6	7	Ruthless

THE BLACK SPOT

OBJECTIVE: To encourage trainees to focus on the context of something.

To get trainees to understand and accept how and why their customers focus on blemishes and imperfections in products and services.

PROCEDURE: Either draw a small black spot on a flip chart, or distribute white sheets of paper with a small black spot to each participant.

Ask a trainee to report what s/he sees on the flip chart (or the sheet). Most often, the respondent will say "A black spot."

Ask a number of other persons the same question, and elicit their responses.

Then affirm to them that you indeed also see a black spot, but note that most individuals overlooked the large white space surrounding it. In the same way, the context around us is often missed or underestimated (as in the organization's culture, or the importance of our interpersonal relationships at work). To paraphrase the poet John Donne, "No person is an island, entire to itself. Therefore, never inquire for whom the bell tolls; it tolls for thee."

Alternatively, you might point out (in customer service training, for example) that customers tend to identify small and large blemishes in our products and services, and many times they have the right to expect them to be fixed.

In conclusion, sometimes it is appropriate that we, too, should look for the "black spot," while at other times we may need to force ourselves to consider the large white area of equal importance.

MATERIALS
REQUIRED: A flip chart or preprinted sheets with black spots on them.

APPROXIMATE
TIME REQUIRED: Five-ten minutes.

SOURCE: Unknown, though inspired by Robert Louis Stevenson's tales of a pirate receiving the "cursed black spot."

V.

COMMUNICATION

AND

LISTENING

DECISIONS, DECISIONS!

OBJECTIVE: To show to participants the desirability of committing themselves to intellectual positions, but only after careful listening for input with which to make potential decisions.

To convince participants of the merits of remaining flexible so as to absorb new inputs and adapt to new rationale.

PROCEDURE: Ask all participants to stand in the center of the room. Quickly share with them a brief scenario that results in a dilemma, or the essence of a controversial topic of contemporary interest. Then state a key assertion flowing from that story. For example, relate the incident from the movie <u>Dead Poets Society</u> in which one of the students wishes to spend some time working in the theater, but his father dictates that he shall not because it would detract from his studies. Assertion: The father's position is defensible. (Many other examples abound, such as abortion, euthanasia, legalization of drugs, etc.)

Designate each corner of the room as space for those who Strongly Agree, Somewhat Agree, Somewhat Disagree, or Strongly Disagree. Ask participants to move to the corner of the room that best represents their current position on the assertion. If they have "No Opinion," they should temporarily stay in the middle of the room, but must eventually choose a corner. (Note: Not all corners will necessarily have someone in them.)

Now ask volunteers from any corner to voice their reasoning. Individuals may, at any time, move from one corner to another, thus indicating that they have changed their mental position on the issue--either directionally (agree--disagree) or by degree (somewhat--strongly).

DISCUSSION QUESTIONS: How flexible are you on controversial issues? Are you truly open to new inputs and arguments?

What kinds of arguments are most effective in swaying opinions?

How can we discipline ourselves to become better listeners?

MATERIALS REQUIRED: None.

**APPROXIMATE
TIME REQUIRED:** 30 minutes.

SOURCE: Judith Briles, Denver, CO.

A READ AND DO TEST

OBJECTIVE: To show, in a humorous way, that people often fail to read and/or follow directions.

PROCEDURE: Distribute a copy of the "Read and Do" test to each participant (see page 171). Ask them to keep the test face down until everyone has a copy. Explain this is a timed test with a maximum time of three minutes allowed to complete the task. Offer no further instructions of any kind. Then state "OK? Ready, set-go!"

MATERIALS
REQUIRED: Copies of the Read and Do test.

APPROXIMATE
TIME REQUIRED: Five minutes.

SOURCE: Unknown.

A READ AND DO TEST

CAN YOU FOLLOW INSTRUCTIONS?

1. Read all that follows before doing anything.
2. Write your name in the upper right-hand-corner of this page.
3. Circle the word "corner" in sentence two.
4. Draw five small squares in upper left hand corner of this page.
5. Put an "X" on each square.
6. Put a circle around each square.
7. Sign your name under line 5.
8. After your name, write "yes, yes, yes."
9. Put a circle around number 7.
10. Put an "X" in the lower-left-hand corner of this page.
11. Draw a triangle around the "X" you just made.
12. Call out your first name when you get to this point in the test.
13. If you think that you have followed directions carefully to this point, call out, "I have!"
14. On the reverse side of this paper add 6950 and 9805.
15. Put a circle around your answer.
16. Count out loud, in your normal speaking voice, from 10 to 1.
17. Put three small pin or pencil holes in the top of this page.
18. If you are the first person to get this far, yell out, "I am the first person to get to this spot and I am the leader in following directions."
19. Say out loud, "I am nearly finished. I have followed directions."
20. Now that you have finished reading carefully, do only those things called for in the sentences numbered 1 and 2. Did you read everything on this page before doing anything?

NOTE: PLEASE BE QUIET AND WATCH THE OTHERS FOLLOW DIRECTIONS.

JUST FOR FUN

OBJECTIVE: To inject humor in discussing problems of communication.

PROCEDURE: Identify that while communication is serious business, we often find humor in strange places. For example, these statements were actually sent to insurance companies:

"An invisible car came out of nowhere, struck my vehicle, and vanished."

"I was on the way to the doctor with rear-end trouble when my universal joint gave way, causing me to have an accident."

"The pedestrian had no idea which direction to go, so I ran over him."

"I collided with a stationary (sic) truck coming the other way."

"I pulled away from the side of the road, glanced at my mother-in-law, and headed over the embankment."

"I had been shopping for plants and was on my way home. As I reached an intersection, a hedge sprang up, obscuring my vision."

"I had been driving my car 40 years when I fell asleep at the wheel and had an accident."

"The other car collided with mine without giving warning of its intentions."

"I thought my window was down, but I found out it was up when I put my hand through it."

"My car was legally parked as it backed into the other vehicle."

"In my attempt to kill a fly, I drove into a telephone pole."

MATERIALS REQUIRED: None.

APPROXIMATE TIME REQUIRED: Three-five minutes.

SOURCE: Varied, including the <u>Toronto Sun</u>.

173

PLENTIFULLY PROVERBS PREACH POETICALLY

OBJECTIVE: To impress upon participants the value of concise, cogent communications, and to provide opportunities to work in task-oriented teams.

PROCEDURE: Distribute to all participants copies of the exercise on page 177. Remind them that a proverb is defined as "a short, pithy saying in frequent and widespread use, expressing a well-known truth or fact."

Ask them to translate each "hidden proverb" into its more commonly known and poetic form. (This can be done individually, or in groups.)

When sufficient time has been provided, randomly call on individuals to disclose their interpretation of what each proverb says. (This can provide a substantial opportunity for levity.)

Engage the group in a debriefing session, in which these answers are shared, and some or all of the discussion questions are used.

1. A fool and his/her money are soon parted.
2. When the cat's away, the mice will play.
3. Too many cooks spoil the broth.
4. Haste makes waste.
5. Crime does not pay.
6. A bird in the hand is worth two in the bush.
7. The early bird gets the worm.
8. Give me liberty or give me death.
9. Better late than never.

DISCUSSION QUESTIONS: Who talks/writes like this in your organization? Why?

What is the impact of such obfuscation (OK, we're guilty, too!) on effective communication?

MATERIALS REQUIRED: Sufficient copies of the "Proverb Simplication Test" for all participants.

APPROXIMATE TIME REQUIRED: 15-20 minutes, depending on the mental alertness of the group.

SOURCE: Various books of common proverbs and folklore.

PROVERB SIMPLICATION EXERCISE

1. An ignoramus and his/her lucre are readily disjoined.

2. In the absence of the feline race, certain small rodents will give themselves up to various pleasurable pastimes.

3. A plethora of culinary specialists vitiate the liquid in which a variety of nutritional substances have been simmered.

4. Impetuous celebrity engenders purposeless spoilage.

5. Illegal transgression has no remuneration for its perpetrators.

6. A winged and feathered animal in the digital limb is as valuable as duet in the shrubbery.

7. The warm-blooded class aves who is governed by promptitude can apprehend the small, elongated, and slender creeping animal.

8. Provide the privilege of affranchisement, or I will feel that life is not worth living.

9. A condition characterized by tardiness is more desirable than one that is systematically marked by eternal absenteeism.

HOW FAST CAN YOU GO?

OBJECTIVE: To demonstrate the importance of understanding basic arithmetic concepts.

To demonstrate that sometimes the form of trainers' questions implies that there is an easy answer, when the trainee should really be challenging the nature of the question itself.

PROCEDURE: Administer "The Orienteering Test" to the participants (see page 181). Tell them to raise their hands as soon as they have the answer.

Ask them for their answers (many will immediately indicate that it is 97.4 mph, which is the sum of 32.4 and 65).

Disclose to them that it is impossible, according to the laws of physics (assuming that your car will not travel at the speed of light), to average 65 mph for the two-lap course once the first lap's average is less than half of that required (e.g., 32.4 mph). This can be demonstrated by using successive calculations of progressively higher speeds for the second lap and averaging them in with the first lap. Note: The common error lies in simply averaging the two lap speeds, and assuming this will create the desired result. However, the calculation must encompass the total distance covered, divided by the total time driven. Therefore, the faster you drive the second lap, the less time it takes, and you can never drive fast enough to create the desired two-lap average time of 65 mph.

DISCUSSION QUESTIONS: How is it that such a seemingly simple arithmetic task can have a hidden meaning to it? What prevented you from seeing its complexity?

What are the implications of the way the problem was posed? (The question suggests that there is an answer, when there is not. The lesson, then, is that participants must learn not to automatically let their minds be closed to other possibilities just by the way the question is stated.)

MATERIALS REQUIRED: Copies of "The Orienteering Test" for all participants.

APPROXIMATE TIME REQUIRED: 15 minutes.

SOURCE: Unknown.

THE ORIENTEERING TEST

DIRECTIONS: Assume that you and your partner have entered a sports-car orienteering contest (This involves completing a defined course by passing certain checkpoints and reaching your prescribed destination while maintaining an assigned <u>average</u> speed. Even minor speed deviations along various sections of the route can result in dramatic consequences for your overall average speed.)

The course consists of two times around a course. You were the driver the first time around, while your partner was the navigator and gave you directions and instructions regarding the pace. Your average speed around the course was 32.4 miles per hour. However, now that you have switched places with your partner and become the navigator, you discover to your dismay that s/he misinterpreted the task, and the average speed required for the two laps is supposed to be <u>65</u> miles per hour. (Fortunately, the course is a very safe one, and your car is capable of sustained speeds of 160 miles per hour.) Question: <u>How fast should you instruct your partner to drive for the next time around the course so as to attain your goal?</u>

_____ mph.

GRUMBLE, GRUMBLE

OBJECTIVE: To provide an opportunity for release of tensions, and to encourage participants to surface negative feelings they may have in a safe way.

To sharpen members' needs for using their listening skills.

PROCEDURE: Pair up all participants.

Instruct participants to talk simultaneously, sharing any complaints, reservations, resentments, grievances, irritants, gripes, or concerns they have on their minds. When one member runs out of issues to disclose, s/he is then to say "grumble, grumble" until all participants are done.

Call a halt to the exercise when it is apparent that the negative energy has dissipated and only superficial "grumbling" is present.

DISCUSSION QUESTIONS:

How did you feel during the exercise? How do you feel now?

Did you feel that you were being "heard" during the exercise?

What are the benefits from this exercise?

What issues do you hear (not report) that you feel merit brief discussion?

Is there any potential application of this process in the workplace?

In what ways do we tend to fall into a "grumble, grumble" trap in our daily conversations? Are these productive?

How did this exercise test your listening skills?

MATERIALS REQUIRED: None.

APPROXIMATE TIME REQUIRED: 10 minutes, plus processing time for any issues to be discussed.

SOURCE: Susan Scott, Lincoln, NB.

FUZZY MEANINGS

OBJECTIVE: To illustrate the wide range of meanings that are often attached to common words and phrases in our language.

PROCEDURE: Identify a list of words and phrases like the following that are commonly used to characterize different degrees or frequencies of events.

a.	Often
b.	Always
c.	Sometimes
d.	Never
e.	Usually
f.	Most of the time
g.	Occasionally
h.	Seldom
i.	A lot
j.	Almost always
k.	Rarely
l.	Frequently
m.	Quite often

Ask participants to specify a number between 0 and 100 that, to them, best indicates the amount (percentage) of time that each word conveys.

Collect the worksheets and tabulate them (e.g., during a break). Calculate the average responses, and note the smallest and highest figure (the range) for each.

Report the result to the group on a flip chart, overhead projector, or handout. Lead a discussion of the results.

DISCUSSION QUESTIONS: What does the data tell you?

Which terms are the most, and least, subject to widely ranging interpretations?

What are the implications for effective communications?

MATERIALS
REQUIRED: Worksheets (preprinted) for each participant; a calculator; and possibly an assistant to help with the calculations.

APPROXIMATE
TIME REQUIRED: Five-ten minutes for administration of the worksheets; ten minutes for distribution of results and discussion of implications.

SOURCE: Jennifer Ramirez, Phoenix, AZ.

LET'S TALK

OBJECTIVE: To demonstrate how quickly people can really get to know others.

PROCEDURE: After the group has been in the session for an hour or two, suggest a method that will allow the group to become better acquainted. Have each person find someone they have not yet met, then tell them they each will have 2 minutes to tell their partners something about themselves. They can talk about anything they want to, e.g., their job, hobby, family, avocation, hometown, etc. Call time at the end of 2 minutes and have the other person do the talking. Call time again at 2 minutes, and ask if anyone would like to tell something about his/her partner (anything unusual, humorous, etc., but not embarrassing).

DISCUSSION QUESTIONS:

How well do you feel you know your partner?

Did you enjoy your 2 minutes of conversation?

How many of your co-workers do you know this well?

Do you have friends or long-time co-workers that you don't know as well as you know your new partner today? Why?

Isn't it curious that most of us haven't taken those 2 minutes with our co-workers? What are some reasons?

MATERIALS REQUIRED: None.

APPROXIMATE TIME REQUIRED: 10-15 minutes.

SOURCE: Austin McGonigle, Marietta, GA.

VI.

PRESENTATION TOOLS

TYING THE KNOT

OBJECTIVE: To sensitize participants to consider trainees' perspectives and needs when giving directions or instructing employees in work methods.

To demonstrate that what you say must be consistent with inputs from other senses (e.g., sight) that the recipient is using.

PROCEDURE: Identify at least four volunteers--people who admit to not knowing how to tie a necktie into a half-windsor knot--and ask them to come to the front of the room.

Give each individual an untied necktie.

a. With one person, have him/her stand facing the audience while you, with your back to him/her, verbally tell them how to tie the tie.

b. With a second person, simply hand him/her the visual illustration of the steps in tying a tie, and let him proceed on his/her own.

c. With a third volunteer, face him/her and have him/her attempt to tie their necktie while you tell him/her and show him/her how.

d. With a fourth volunteer, stand side by side with him/her (facing the same direction) while you "show and tell" him/her how to tie the tie.

DISCUSSION QUESTIONS: Which method seemed to work the best? Why?

Why didn't the other methods work as well?

What lessons or learning principles could effectively be incorporated into instruction of this kind?

MATERIALS REQUIRED: A small number of old neckties; the illustration showing how to tie the knot.

APPROXIMATE TIME REQUIRED: 10-20 minutes, depending on the number of volunteers and other instructional approaches used.

SOURCE: Unknown.

TYING A HALF-WINDSOR KNOT

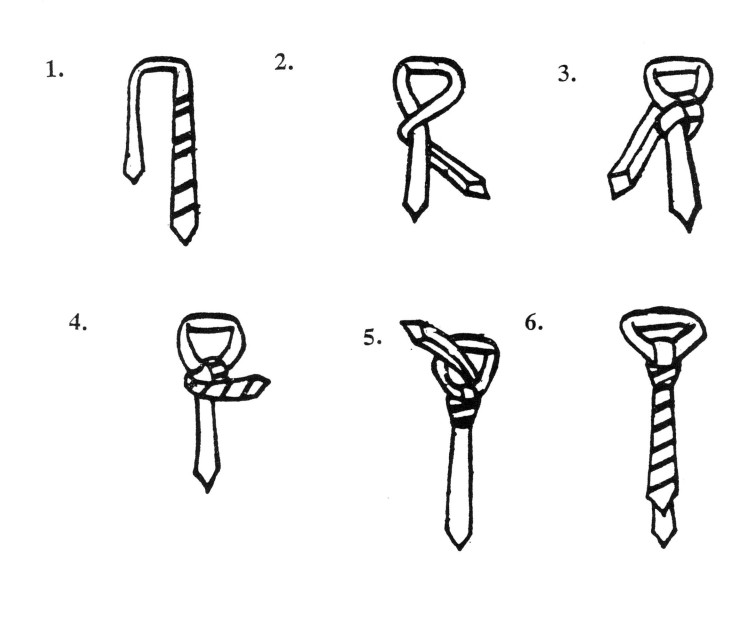

THE "NO-BELL" PRIZE WINNER

OBJECTIVE: To provide a humorous (albeit groan-inducing) means for introducing a speaker (including a self-introduction).

PROCEDURE: Announce to the participants at the beginning of a program that the next speaker had recently spoken to a local Rotary Club (or any local group). As part of the introduction today, you would like to share the club members' reactions to the speaker with the group.

The club uses a brass bell for many purposes--to call the group to attention, to signal the end of the meeting, to announce major events on their agenda, etc. They also use a bell system to rate the guest speaker that they have at each of their meetings. It works like this:

a.   If the speaker was truly spectacular, s/he receives a four-bell rating (and the bell is struck four times).

b.   If the speaker was very good, s/he receives a three-bell rating (and the bell is struck three times).

c.   If the speaker was average, s/he receives a two-bell rating (and the bell is struck two times).

d.   If the speaker was only marginal, s/he receives a one-bell rating (and the bell is struck once).

Of course, the rating system is secret so as not to embarrass the speaker. A designated evaluator simply makes the decision at the end to the program and then strikes the bell the appropriate number of times.

In the recent appearance before this local Rotary Club, you are pleased to announce that you (or the speaker you are now introducing to the program) were the only person in the club's 73-year history to receive the No-bell prize for public speaking! (So please welcome today our very own No-bell speaker, Mr/Ms...................!)

MATERIALS REQUIRED: None.

APPROXIMATE TIME REQUIRED: Three-five minutes.

SOURCE: Unknown.

195

THE STANDING OVATION

OBJECTIVE: To provide a bit of levity to the beginning of a program.

PROCEDURE: Walk into the room in which the participants are assembled.

Invite everyone to stand up and spread out (approximately an arm's length apart).

Tell them that to make sure they are awake and receptive to the forthcoming material in your session, you will lead them in an exercise designed to help get their blood moving more rapidly, and stimulate the nerve endings in their hands.

Direct them to stretch their arms out at their sides (horizontally from their bodies). When they have all done so properly, then ask them to rapidly bring their hands together, then back to their sides (repeating the two-step sequence about 10 times in rapid succession).

Conclude by telling the group that you aren't sure how much better they feel now, but that you feel really good, because this is the first time in all your years of training/presenting that you have begun a session to a standing ovation!

MATERIALS REQUIRED: None.

APPROXIMATE TIME REQUIRED: Three-five minutes.

SOURCE: Lee Beckner, Provo, UT.

LEADER OF THE BAND

OBJECTIVE: To provide an opportunity for participants to loosen up after a period of intense activity, discussion, or passive absorption of a lecture or video.

PROCEDURE: Pick a time when the group's energy seems particularly low.

Call for a unique (non-coffee, non-use of restroom) break. Ask all participants to stand up and make sufficient room around themselves so as not interfere with free movement of their arms.

Tell them that they have won the right to be "The Leader of the Band" and therefore direct the world-famous Philadelphia Orchestra (for the next five minutes). You might also wish to tell them that mock-direction of an orchestra is believed to be excellent emotional release and physical (cardiovascular) exercise. Then play a selection and ask them all to simultaneously lead the orchestra.

Note: This works best if you have carefully selected the music. We recommend that the music be familiar to all, so they will know what is coming next. The music should be relatively fast-paced to stimulate energetic directing (Sousa marches, or even Strauss waltzes work well); also, music with a variety of speeds and volumes also tends to elicit different directing styles.

DISCUSSION
QUESTIONS: How do you feel now that you have directed the orchestra?

How many of you are likely to go home and direct music from your own record collection?

What is there about the activity of orchestra-directing that gives us permission to wave our arms and move our bodies in a refreshing way--something we would otherwise not be inclined to do?

MATERIALS
REQUIRED: Tape recorder and player.

APPROXIMATE
TIME REQUIRED: Five minutes.

SOURCE: Art Richardson, Le Mars, IA.

I'M GLAD I'M HERE

OBJECTIVE: To start the training program with a positive and humorous opening.

PROCEDURE: Immediately after the introduction, tell the group that you're glad to be there also! To prove that, go around the room asking, "If you weren't here today, what would you be doing that you're glad you don't have to?" Keep the answers light and fast moving.

MATERIALS REQUIRED: 10 minutes.

SOURCE: Sue Hotchkiss, City of Phoenix, Phoenix, AZ.

WHAT YOU STROKE IS WHAT YOU GET

OBJECTIVE: To demonstrate to supervisors and others that "whatever behaviors they reinforce will tend to be repeated."

To convince supervisors and others that reinforcement is not necessarily expensive.

PROCEDURE: Initiate any type of group discussion, or request for idea generation.

As each participant responds, distribute something to that individual. This may be an oreo cookie, a candy bar, an engraved pencil with a motivational slogan, a bumper sticker, a coffee mug, an engraved decorative pin or ribbon, or even a T-shirt. (For variety, if someone gives a patentedly incorrect or inappropriate response, pull out a toy cap gun and pretend to "shoot" the individual. Make sure that everyone present is aware that it is a cap pistol, of course). You may also choose to ignore someone's response on occasion.

DISCUSSION QUESTIONS: What is the difference between a reward and a reinforcement? Hint: A reward is a speculative, potential reinforcement; a reinforcer is one that you have strong reason to believe will act so as to provide satisfaction to the recipient, and elicit future similar desirable behavior.

How did you feel when you received a reinforcer (even a relatively trivial one)? What determined your relative degree of satisfaction with what you received? How did you feel when you did not get reinforced for a comment?

What reinforcers could you use at work for your employees? Do you have an adequate budget to allow you to do so?

MATERIALS REQUIRED: Whatever items are chosen for demonstration purposes (e.g., cookies).

APPROXIMATE TIME REQUIRED: 15 minutes.

SOURCE: Various, including Bob Pike.

GUEST SPEAKER INTRODUCTION

OBJECTIVE: To introduce a guest speaker (VIP, etc.) in a novel way.

PROCEDURE: Secure a copy of the guest speaker or trainer's bio or introduction. Actually cut up the sheet and distribute to several participants in advance so each has a sentence or two to read or memorize.

When you bring up the guest speaker, state; "Our guest is such a celebrity, I'll bet you know more about him/her than I do." Then, on cue, the participants relate something about that person's background.

**MATERIALS
REQUIRED:**   Guest speaker or trainer's bio.

**APPROXIMATE
TIME REQUIRED:** Two-three minutes.

SOURCE: Unknown.

ALTERNATIVES TO "SHUT UP!"

OBJECTIVE: To suggest alternative approaches that trainers can use to quiet down a group or redirect their attention to the trainer following a period of small-group discussion. The following are a variety of methods used effectively by various trainers.

PROCEDURE: One of the most effective methods is to depersonalize the process of quieting down the group. In other words, to avoid verbal comments (e.g., "May I have your attention, please," or "will you please quiet down now?") Instead, acquire and use some impersonal device that acts as a cue or signal to the group, and to which all have agreed. Examples of such devices include a simple whistle, an old-fashioned school bell, an oven or even a small musical instrument (e.g., a recorder, triangle, harmonica, or kazoo).

Nonverbal signals can work equally well. For years the Boy Scouts of America have effectively used a simple three-fingered boy scout salute as an "everybody quiet" cue. The trainer only needs to catch one group's attention with a signal like this, and then the responsibility for spreading the message becomes shared by other group members.

Some trainers play a recognizable theme song on a cassette recorder.

Some trainers create three cue cards (e.g., 3-2-1, or green light-amber light-red light) that they simply display prominently to the group as a nonverbal signal to indicate the remaining time available.

Another possibility is to announce to the assembled participants at the beginning of the session that you will tell your best humorous stories in the first minute following every coffee break and small group session. However, you will speak very softly, so that only those who are quiet can hear the stories!

MATERIALS REQUIRED: Any of the items selected in the procedures above.

APPROXIMATE TIME REQUIRED: Virtually none.

SOURCE: Bob Pike, Eden Prairie, MN, and others.

THE GREAT TRAINING SPELL-DOWN

OBJECTIVE: To utilize expectations, peer competition, and social facilitation to reinforce and accent familiarity with, and retention of, key terms introduced in the training session.

PROCEDURE: Announce at the beginning of a training session, that a contest will be held at the end to determine the champion speller in the group. All words will come from terminology introduced or used within the training program.

If feasible, provide written materials as the program progresses in which key terms are introduced and defined.

If the group is large and/or time is tight, prepare a written preliminary test to administer to the entire group. Collect the tests, score them, and use the results to screen the group down to a manageable number of finalists (e.g., 2-10 persons). Ask them to stand in front of the room, and ask each of them in turn to spell a word from a master list you have prepared in advance. If they miss one, they must sit down. When only two remain, the winner is determined by who can spell the other person's missed word, as well as the next word on the list. Some prizes might be offered for the winner, of course.

DISCUSSION QUESTIONS: How will this exercise help you to remember the terms in the future?

What would you do differently next time you had the opportunity to participate?

What were the positive and negative impacts of having to perform (spell) in front of others?

MATERIALS REQUIRED: Previously prepared list of terms; answer sheets for the orally administered pretest to screen contestants; one or more prizes for the top competitors.

APPROXIMATE TIME REQUIRED: 20-30 minutes, depending on the number of participants, their spelling capabilities, and the difficulty level of the terms chosen.

SOURCE: Unknown.

210

LEGITIMIZING LEVITY

OBJECTIVE: To stimulate people's creativity about the subject at hand.

To legitimize the use of humor within the training context.

PROCEDURE: Briefly introduce or provide an overview of a topic. Outline the key points to be covered, but don't get into any details.

Before getting specific on policy, procedures, or recommendations about how to do something, ask the participants to brainstorm all the humorous/impractical or unwise ways of achieving the desired goal.

Example: In a seminar on time management, participants may offer suggestions for saving time (using it more efficiently), such as these:

a. Cut your phone cord.
b. Shorten the front legs of your office's visitor's chair, so guests will unconsciously feel uncomfortable (like sliding off) and leave sooner.
c. Burn all but the first pieces of mail to arrive daily.
d. Have Domino's Pizza deliver lunch to you in your office.
e. Get an unlisted phone number.

Once everyone has had a few good laughs, you can easily make a transition to your regular and more serious agenda for the day.

**MATERIALS
REQUIRED:**   None.

**APPROXIMATE
TIME REQUIRED:** 15 minutes.

SOURCE: Varied, including Alan Lakein.

VII.

CONFERENCE

LEADERSHIP

ACTION AUCTION

OBJECTIVE: To encourage participant's oral involvement during training sessions.

To encourage participants to share their physical/financial/personal resources with trainers.

PROCEDURE: Distribute a basic amount of play money (e.g., $500 each) to participants as they enter the training session. (This will pique their curiosity.)

A little while later, explain the auction process to them:

a.   Some auction items are already available (e.g., the company has donated a book related to the course being taught; a T-shirt or baseball cap with the company logo on it; a motivational audio tape.)

b.   Participants are invited to donate other items to the auction (These could range from tangible items like products they have available, to less tangible items like the creation of a hand-lettered certificate, a back/foot massage or a tennis lesson.) They should be urged to be creative, and contribute at least one item per person.

c.   Announce that additional money can be earned throughout the training session/meeting by active (and high-quality) participation. Then begin rewarding such participation by spontaneously distributing play money to those who become involved as the day progresses.

d.   Collect the contributed items, announce what they will be (a typed list is preferred so they will know how to allocate their money), and conduct the auction.

**MATERIALS
REQUIRED:**   Play money of large denominations sufficient to distribute to all participants; some basic auction items donated by the presenter and/or the employer.

APPROXIMATE
TIME REQUIRED: Five-ten minutes to announce the exercise, call for contributions, and explain how additional money may be acquired. From 30-60 minutes for actual conduct of the auction, depending on number of items, minimum raises of bids, number of participants, and intensity of the bidding.

SOURCE: Region 6 ASTD Conference.

AND YOUR RECORDER IS...

OBJECTIVE: To identify several ways the trainer can select a group recorder or reporter for small-group discussions.

PROCEDURE: Announce any date at random. The person whose birthday is closest to that date becomes the recorder.

Select a person who lives closest (or farthest) from the meeting site.

Select a person wearing red (or any other color).

Select a person with the most children.

Everyone puts his/her right forefinger in the air. At your signal, point to the person at your table you want to be the recorder. (The person with most "votes," wins.)

Select the person newest (or oldest) to the organization.

**MATERIALS
REQUIRED:** None.

**APPROXIMATE
TIME REQUIRED:** One minute.

SOURCE: Varied, including Bob Pike, Eden Prairie, MN.

EXPERT EXPERIENCES (E2)

OBJECTIVE:

To identify who, within a training group, has relevant experiences to share with the other participants.

To alert other participants to the value of prior relevant experiences.

To provide appropriate recognition to individuals with experience, and to indicate the value of their participation.

PROCEDURE:

Ask participants to write down a significant personal experience that they have had in the subject area. It may be either positive or negative--simply a notable occurrence from which a lesson was derived.

Divide the participants into discussion groups of approximately five persons each. Ask them to share their experiences with each other.

Ask each group to select the two most relevant experiences that were presented at their table.

A team spokesperson should report to the entire group on the experiences that were selected. Key-word summaries can be written by the group facilitator and posted on the wall. (If desired, contributor names can be attached to each experience for later reference.)

What experiences of those listed have the greatest potential bearing on our subject today?

Which single one is the most important lesson for you to recall? (Note: If desired, a simple prize can be awarded to the originator of the winning idea to provide appropriate recognition.)

Paper for each participant, a flip chart pad mounted on an easel, marking pens, masking tape, and a possible prize.

TE
[RED: 30 minutes.

Eugene C. Fetteroll, Jr., Boston, MA.

Fredy-Jo Grafman
Principal

GRAFMAN & ASSOCIATES

160 Vassar Road · Bala Cynwyd, PA 19004

(610) 667-5059

MIX OR MATCH

OBJECTIVE: To provide a series of options for expeditiously creating newly mixed groups within a training setting.

To preplan the process of creating different sized groups.

PROCEDURE: Determine how many participants you will have in the training group.

Assess how many different mixtures of participants you will need throughout the training session, and how many persons you want in each subgroup.

List the participants on a worksheet similar to the example on the page 223. Then progressively assign a number, letter, symbol, color, product name, or other differentiating characteristics to each member. Note that you can create varying numbers of groups, and varying subgroup sizes in this fashion.

When creating tags or tent cards, simply code them with this information (e.g., Maria Santiago #3, B, yellow, Toasted Granola Flakes.)

Whenever you need to establish new task-oriented or discussion groups, simply instruct all the "yellows" (blues, reds, etc.) to get together. Next time, instruct all the 1s to join together, etc.

Note: If you fail to prepare enough preplanned mixtures and need a newly mixed group, simply ask them to form new groups that have no two symbols alike (e.g., a square, circle, triangle, arrow all in the same group).

MATERIALS REQUIRED: Name cards or tent cards; advance worksheet.

APPROXIMATE TIME REQUIRED: Two minutes for each new group to form, once directions are given.

SOURCE: John Newstrom, Duluth, MN.

MIX OR MATCH WORKSHEET (SAMPLE)

NAME	#	LETTER	SYMBOL	COLOR	OTHER
Anna	1	E	Square	Blue	
Bob	2	A	Circle	Red	
Carole	3	B	Triangle	Yellow	
Duffy	4	C	Arrow	Blue	
Elaine	5	D	Square	Red	
Fosdick	6	E	Circle	Yellow	
Greg	1	A	Triangle	Blue	
Heidi	2	B	Arrow	Red	
Ida	3	C	Square	Yellow	
Jorge	4	D	Circle	Blue	
Keith	5	E	Triangle	Red	
Lori	6	A	Arrow	Yellow	
Maria	1	B	Square	Blue	
Nils	2	C	Circle	Red	
Opal	3	D	Triangle	Yellow	
Pete	4	E	Arrow	Blue	
Quincy	5	A	Square	Red	
Roxy	6	B	Circle	Yellow	

PASSWORD REVIEW

OBJECTIVE: To assess the degree of retention of key concepts among a group of trainees.

To reinforce major terms at the end of a training session (or module).

PROCEDURE: Develop a master set of key vocabulary terms associated with the training program.

Print each on a separate card, and create a duplicate deck. Number the cards sequentially to assure that they remain in order.

Divide the group into two teams. Select the first two players, one from each team. They should each draw the top card (a similar one) but not show it to their teammates. One player starts first, by giving a verbal clue (e.g., a rhyming word, a synonym, a single-word clue) to the teammates. The teammates, in collaboration, may make one guess within a short, fixed time period. If they are correct, they get 10 points. If they are incorrect, the second team's player may offer a new clue, and that team's players get a chance to guess for 9 possible points. Play continues on the word until 10 guesses are made, or the term has been guessed. Points are recorded for the team with the correct guess, and play continues to the next set of players and words in the deck. The team with the greatest number of points at the end of a given time period (or the deck) wins, and may be given a prize of some nature.

DISCUSSION QUESTIONS: Which terms gave the group the greatest difficulty? Why?

Which terms would you now like to have clarified?

APPROXIMATE TIME REQUIRED: Totally dependent on the number of terms, familiarity of the players with the terms, time limit placed on each guessing round, and the players' clue-giving capacity.

SOURCE: Unknown.

VIII.

CREATIVE

PROBLEM

SOLVING

BRAINSTORMING REVISITED

OBJECTIVE: To clear the cobwebs in group work and acclimate participants to a creative process.

PROCEDURE: Although "brainstorming" has been around since Alex Osborne's introduction of this technique in the 1950s, it seems now to be regaining popularity after many years of dormancy.

Since many participants have never been exposed to this novel approach to problem solving, review and describe the four rules of brainstorming:

No critical judgement is allowed.

Quantity, not quality, is desired.

The wilder the better!

Hitch-hiking (combination and improvement) are sought.

To get participants in a creative mode, it is suggested that a "warm-up" exercise be used. For example, small groups of 3-4 are formed and participants are asked to think of different uses for a paper-clip. Announce they have just 60 seconds, and have someone jot down the number of ideas their group suggests. (Don't write out the actual ideas.) Following this exercise, address the real-world problem to attack.

**MATERIALS
REQUIRED:** None.

**APPROXIMATE
TIME REQUIRED:** 12-15 minutes.

SOURCE: Unknown.

WHAT IF...

OBJECTIVE: To allow participants to prepare contingency plans for potentially serious or disastrous situations.

PROCEDURE: After a brief review of the rules of brainstorming (no criticism; quantity, not quality; etc.), tell the group they will now get some practice in handling future problems.

Ask the group to think of a recent situation they had either experienced or observed that featured "Murphy's Law." Form triads and have each group agree on one real-world problem (e.g., "the PA set didn't work; the handout materials didn't arrive; the airline lost all my overheads").

Select one group to pose their problem ("What if the speaker doesn't show up?") and throw the nerfball to another group. Whoever catches it must offer some possible solutions. (If necessary, allow other participants to also offer viable answers). That group then states its problem ("What If...") and tosses the ball to another group. Continue as time allows.

**MATERIALS
REQUIRED:** Nerfball.

**APPROXIMATE
TIME REQUIRED:** 15-25 minutes.

SOURCE: Unknown.

SQUARE WITHIN A SQUARE

OBJECTIVE: To legitimize the process of asking for help and assistance and reinforcing others for their learning and progress.

PROCEDURE: Give each participant exactly 24 toothpicks. Ask them to arrange them in the pattern shown on page 235 (four rows of three each; four columns of three each; result is nine adjacent small squares).

Ask them to each remove eight toothpicks so that the result will be the formation of only two squares (which may be of different size).

Tell them that if they have difficulty solving the task, they may nonverbally signal a request for corroboration of a potentially correct move by raising their hand. If they are proposing a correct move, respond with a loud and enthusiastic "Yes!" or several quick band-claps. Otherwise, simply give a quiet "No."

When participants have completed the entire task successfully, they may also become "consultants", providing feedback and reinforcement to those still working. Consequently, by the end of the process, a large number of people may be available to clap for the successful moves of the last participant.

KEY: Remove the eight toothpicks that surround the smallest square in the center. This leaves a 4-toothpick square and the exterior 12-toothpick square, or a "square-within-a-square."

DISCUSSION QUESTIONS: How many of you asked for help? How did you feel when you had to ask for assistance? How comfortable are you doing so in other contexts? What prevents or inhibits you from doing so?

How did you feel when you made a right move and received a round of applause (clapping) for doing so? How did you feel when you were successful and became a consultant with the opportunity to assist others?

MATERIALS REQUIRED: 24 toothpicks (precounted and bundled) per person.

**APPROXIMATE
TIME REQUIRED:** 10-15 minutes.

SOURCE: J. J. Cochran, Minneapolis, MN.

KEY: Square-within-a-Square

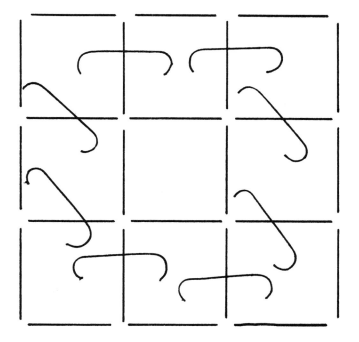

ALPHABET SOUP

OBJECTIVE: To allow participants some practice in simple problem solving.

PROCEDURE: Prepare the following questions as a quickie quiz. Ask participants to complete the exercise as quickly as possible.

1.   What is the only letter open on all sides?

2.   What is the only curved letter that is the same upside down?

3.   What are the only letters containing one single horizontal line?

4.   What is the only letter with two parallel horizontal lines?

5.   What is the only letter with two diagonal straight lines?

6.   Abecedarians who mind their P's and Q's should have little trouble with this puzzle: What letters of the alphabet are:

    a.   a bird?
    b.   part of your head?
    c.   an insect?
    d.   a drink?
    e.   a building extension?
    f.   a hint?
    g.   a vegetable?
    h.   a body of water?
    i.   a farm animal?

MATERIALS REQUIRED: Handout sheets.

APPROXIMATE TIME REQUIRED: Five minutes.

SOURCE: Varied.

238

ALPHABET SOUP

1. X
2. S
3. H, L and T
4. Z
5. X

a. J
b. I
c. B
d. T
e. L
f. Q
g. P
h. C
i. U

PROBLEM SOLVING THROUGH SYNERGISM
(Five-Square Configuration)

OBJECTIVE: To demonstrate that together there is greater total effect than the sum of the individual efforts.

PROCEDURE: Form teams of 5-8 participants. Each team is given a set of figures as shown on page 243. Their task is to arrange the figures into 5 squares so that at least one side of each square touches and is in line with one side of another square. Use 5 squares each time.

**MATERIALS
REQUIRED:** One game sheet, for each team participant.

**APPROXIMATE
TIME REQUIRED:** 10-15 minutes.

SOURCE: Joe Romiti, IBM, Charlotte, NC.

FIVE-SQUARE CONFIGURATION

1. Arrange five squares so that at least one side of each
    square touches and is in line with one side of another square.

2. There are 12 possible configurations.

3. Utilize all five squares each time.

4. Mirror images are not acceptable.

EXAMPLE:

THERE ARE ELEVEN MORE...... GOOD LUCK!!!!!!!

5-SQUARE ANSWERS

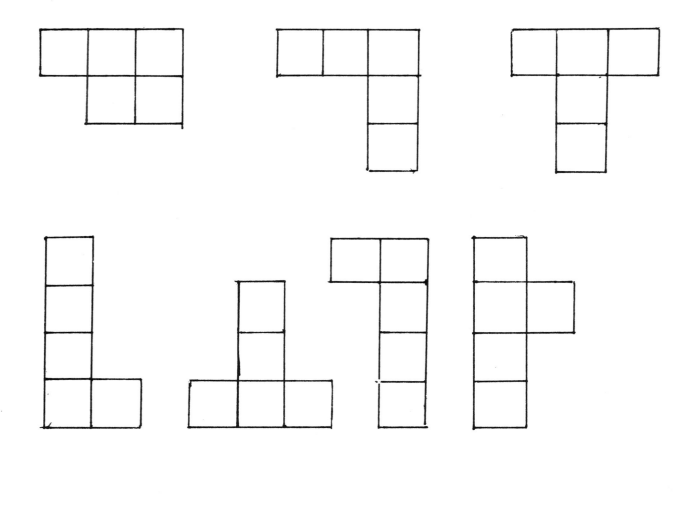

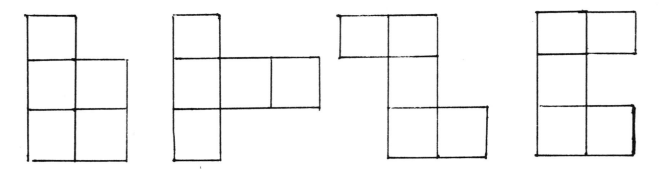

WORK SMARTER, NOT HARDER!

OBJECTIVE: To stimulate participants to search for better ways of doing things (e.g., work simplications).

PROCEDURE: Select a basic task of some kind for demonstration purposes. Examples could be a pegboard with fifty holes (five rows of ten holes, coded by five colors) and fifty pegs of the same five colors to be placed in matching rows on the peg board; a fifty-piece jigsaw puzzle to be constructed; a sack of varicolored poker chips to sort and place into a rack in single-colored columns, etc.

Ask for a volunteer to time you while you engage in the task in a relatively (but not obviously foot-dragging) inefficient way.

Ask for small teams of individuals to develop plans for how to make the process more efficient (e.g., through better material organization, better placement of "raw materials," more efficient movement, or use of teamwork.) Give them about 15 minutes to prepare their proposals.

Call on a team to explain its proposals to the whole group. Then ask for a volunteer from another team to try out the ideas, while elapsed time is again recorded. Repeat for as many groups as you have time for, recording the results each time.

DISCUSSION QUESTIONS: What are the general principles that you implicitly applied in your proposals that seemed to have the greatest impact?

Is work simplication a problem-solving process, or a mind-set? Or both?

What is the motivational effect of competition (e.g., trying to beat instructor in this case) on performance?

MATERIALS REQUIRED: Pegboard and pegs; jigsaw puzzle; or other demonstration exercises.

APPROXIMATE TIME REQUIRED: 20-30 minutes.

SOURCE: Ed Fry, Phoenix, AZ.

TRIANGULATING ON TRIANGLES

OBJECTIVE: To discourage trainees from jumping to early conclusions before careful analysis of the total picture from many angles (pun intended).

PROCEDURE: Break the group into teams of three (basis for the ensuing process of "triangulating"--looking at something from three different directions in hopes of increasing the accuracy of the product.)

Instruct the teams to count the number of triangles portrayed in the figure (shown on page 251). After a few minutes, ask for teams to report on how many they found in the diagram, and an explanation of which ones they are.

Before disclosing the number of triangles, ask them to examine the effectiveness of their team experience. What did they do well, and what could they have improved upon?

Then proceed to inform them that there are a total of 47, as follows: ACE FBD, AED, AEH, AEB, AFC, AFH, AFD, AFB, FEB, FCE, FEJ, FEH, DEA, DEB, DEH, DEG, DEF, DCH, DCA, DCB, ECH, ECB, ECF, ACH, ACD, AFC, ABG, ABH, ABD, BCI, BCH, BCF, BGH, BHI, HID, HJD, HJF, HFG, FED, FHD, FBJ, BJD, BFH, BHD, FID, FGD.

DISCUSSION QUESTIONS: What factors inhibit you from seeing all 47 triangles?

How does a systematic approach to identifying the triangles help (e.g., the triangles originating from a single side; or first identifying the number of single triangles)?

How does working in a team of individuals help you to "see" things from different angles?

MATERIALS REQUIRED: A copy of the diagram for each participant (or at least one for each team).

APPROXIMATE TIME REQUIRED: 10-15 minutes.

SOURCE: Unknown.

THE HIDDEN TRIANGLES FIGURE

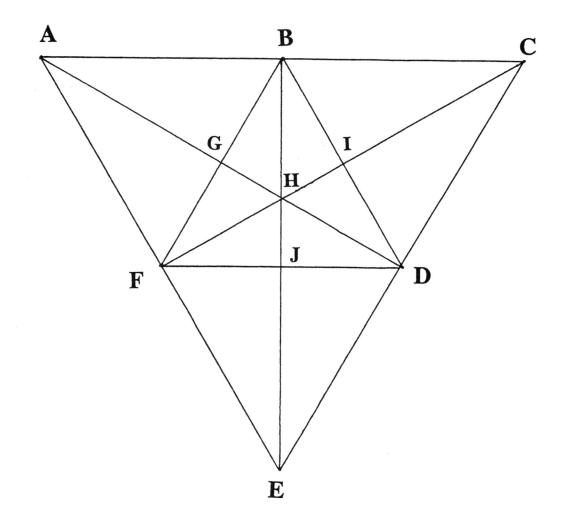

252

ONE STEP AT A TIME

OBJECTIVE: To let people use their powers of creativity and logic.

PROCEDURE: Ask the group to call out a series of word-nouns. Write the first 10 nouns on the left-side column (Column 1) of a flip chart or overhead. As the group <u>randomly</u> identifies 10 more, write these in the far right (see figure on page 255) column (Column 5). Their task is to compare the word in the far left column with the noun in the right column. Fill in the additional three spaces so that each word is somehow logically related to the one on its left. The last word in the far right column need not have any relationship with Column 1, only to the word immediately preceding it.

For example:

Column 1	2	3	4	Column 5
Trainer	_____	_____	_____	TV set

POSSIBLE SOLUTION:

Column 1	2	3	4	Column 5
Trainer	Flip chart	AV	Video	TV set

MATERIALS REQUIRED: Flip chart, and/or handouts as shown on page 255.

APPROXIMATE TIME REQUIRED: 10 minutes.

SOURCE: Unknown.

ONE STEP AT A TIME

DIRECTIONS: As nouns are randomly called out, write these words in Column 1. Then write ten additional nonrelated nouns in Column 5. Your task is to fill in the three blank lines with a new word that is logically related or associated with the one immediately preceding it. Keep in mind your goal is to logically reach Column 5. Remember, the final word need not be related to Column 1, only Column 4.

EXAMPLE:

Column 1	2	3	4	Column 5
TRAINER	_____	_____	_____	TV SET
_____	_____	_____	_____	_____
_____	_____	_____	_____	_____
_____	_____	_____	_____	_____
_____	_____	_____	_____	_____
_____	_____	_____	_____	_____
_____	_____	_____	_____	_____
_____	_____	_____	_____	_____
_____	_____	_____	_____	_____
_____	_____	_____	_____	_____
_____	_____	_____	_____	_____

THE NEXT DIMENSION

OBJECTIVE: To encourage trainees to stretch their minds beyond their current capacities.

PROCEDURE: Provide each participant with six toothpicks (or similar items such as pencils, or stir sticks) of equal length.

Instruct each participant to construct four equilateral triangles from the materials provided.

COMMENT: Most individuals will begin by laying the toothpicks on their work surface in various arrangements, resulting in perhaps two adjacent triangles sharing a common side, or a square divided into four nonequilateral triangles (the two intersecting toothpicks will not reach all the way from corner to corner, however).

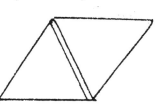

KEY: The key to successful completion of the task is to break out of one's natural tendency to think simply (in two dimensions) and move into a new dimension--the third. When this is done (or this clue is provided) most participants will be able to construct four equilateral triangles by creating a triangles and by running the remaining three from a corner of the base to a peak, as shown on page 259.

DISCUSSION QUESTIONS: What factors limited your ability to solve this puzzle initially?

How can "thinking in a new dimension" help you solve future problems?

MATERIALS REQUIRED: Sufficient toothpicks for each participant (six for each participant).

APPROXIMATE TIME REQUIRED: Five minutes.

SOURCE: Catherine A. Arther, Liberty, TX.

KEY: THE NEXT DIMENSION

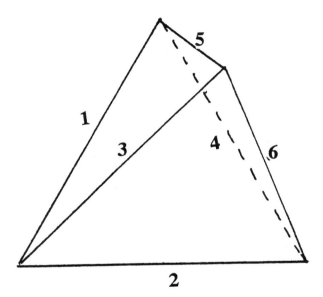

EQUATION QUIZ

OBJECTIVE: To be used at the start of a session, or to "shift gears" to a different module of instruction.

PROCEDURE: Distribute copies of this page. Each item below represents an equation, acronym or well-known phrase.

1. 1 = R.A. in E.B.
2. 10 = L.I.
3. 3 = L.K. that L.T.M.
4. 4 = S. on a V.
5. 5 = T. on a C. (including S. in T.)
6. 6 = P. on a P.T.
7. 7 = Y. of B.L. for B. a M.
8. 2 = G. of V.
9. 9 = J. of the S.C.
10. 10 = D. in a T.N. (including the A.C.)
11. 76 = T. that L. the B.P.
12. 20 = C. in a P.
13. 3 = S.Y.O. at the O.B.G.
14. 66 = B. of the B. (in the K.J.V.)
15. 15 = M. on a D.M.C.
16. 20 = Q. (A., V., or M.)
17. 7 = D. with S.W.
18. 30 = S. over T.
19. 8 = D. a W. (in the B.S.)
20. 2,000 = P. in a T.

MATERIALS REQUIRED: Copies of this page.

APPROXIMATE TIME REQUIRED: Five-eight minutes.

SOURCE: Unknown.

ANSWERS

1. 1 = Rotten Apple in Every Barrel

2. 10 = Little Indians

3. 3 = Little Kittens that Lost Their Mittens

4. 4 = Strings on a Violin

5. 5 = Tires on a Car (including the Spare in the Trunk)

6. 6 = Pockets on a Pool Table

7. 7 = Years of Bad Luck for Breaking a Mirror

8. 2 = Gentlemen of Verona

9. 9 = Justices of the Supreme Court

10. 10 = Digits in a Telephone Number (including the Area Code)

11. 76 = Trombones that Led the Big Parade

12. 20 = Cigarettes in a Pack

13. 3 = Strikes and You're Out at the Old Ball Game

14. 66 = Books of the Bible (in the King James Version)

15. 15 = Men on a Dead Man's Chest

16. 20 = Questions (Animal, Vegetable, or Mineral)

17. 7 = Dwarfs with Snow White

18. 30 = Seconds over Tokyo

19. 8 = Days a Week (in the Beatles Song)

20. 2,000 = Pounds in a Ton

MAKING WORK LIKE PLAY

OBJECTIVE: To demonstrate the value, and ease, of using knowledge in one area to assist in solving problems in another domain.

To demonstrate the need to break out of traditional ways of viewing something (e.g., work) so as to more constructively and objectively approach a task.

PROCEDURE: Lead a brief discussion of "play" vs. "work." What are different connotations of each? For example, what does it mean to "play the piano" for a 9-year old vs. a concert pianist? Or "playing tennis" for a weekend tennis player vs. a touring professional tennis player?

What are the major characteristics of play that make it so motivating to its participants? (Items generated can be listed on a transparency or flip chart. They will likely match the list provided fairly closely).

Form small discussion groups of 3-5 persons each. Assign each group a different set (e.g., a small number) of the statements on the following page to work on. Tell them that their task is to indicate how "work" can be made more like the elements of "play" shown there. (For example, night-shift crews and day-shift crews can compete for prizes; or winning performers can be named "Employees of the Month.")

DISCUSSION QUESTIONS: What are the major implications of this exercise for managers?

What prevents managers from making work more like play? Are these forces real, or imagined?

What would be the likely (positive and negative) results of making work more like play? Could others in the organization accept such creative behaviors?

MATERIALS REQUIRED: None, unless you wish to use the list provided on page 267.

APPROXIMATE TIME REQUIRED: 30-60 minutes.

SOURCE: Father A. J. Foley, via Dr. Richard K. Gaumnitz.

COMPARING PLAY AND WORK

FEATURES OF PLAY	APPLICATIONS TO WORK
1. Alternatives are available.	1.
2. New games can be played on different days.	2.
3. Contact with equals, friends, peers.	3.
4. Flexibility of choosing teammates.	4.
5. Flexible duration of play.	5.
6. Flexible time of when to play.	6.
7. Opportunity to be/express oneself.	7.
8. Opportunity to use one's talents.	8.
9. Skillful play brings applause, praise, and recognition from spectators.	9.
10. Healthy competition, rivalry, and challenge exists.	10.
11. Opportunity for social interaction.	11.
12. Opportunity for on-going teams to develop.	12.
13. Mechanisms for scoring one's performance are available (feedback).	13.
14. Rules assure basic fairness & justice.	14.
15. Playing involves experiences of achievement, thrill of winning, handling losing with grace, etc.	15.

IT'LL NEVER FLY, WILBUR!

OBJECTIVE: To allow participants to identify possible roadblocks or barriers that might impede new policies or procedures.

PROCEDURE: In introducing a new concept, a plan of action, or a problem-solving session, the facilitator sets the stage by identifying the objectives of the session. For example, "Our task this morning is to identify ways to increase customer service in each of our departments."

Then participants are immediately asked to write out 4-5 problems they see that would possibly block the organization from achieving the goal. For example, "we don't have time to train our people," or "we can't take people off the line," or "we can't afford to bring in a Customer Service consultant."

Subdivide the audience into groups of 3-4 and ask them to discuss their concerns. Then, each subgroup writes out its 3 major roadblocks on a 3 x 5 card and reports them to the entire group. Facilitator acknowledges comments and redistributes the 3 x 5 cards so each subgroup receives a different card.

Subgroups' next task is to attack the problem roadblocks and creatively think of several ways to solve them. They then report back to the entire group.

MATERIALS REQUIRED: Flip chart, 3 x 5 cards.

APPROXIMATE TIME REQUIRED: 20-30 minutes.

SOURCE: Unknown.

THE PARLOR GAME

OBJECTIVE: To speed up any process involving recognition or familiarity.

PROCEDURE: Group people in to teams of five to eight. Assemble up to 30 portable objects related to your training (examples could be computer parts, technical items, tools, manuals, forms, supplies, materials, office equipment, etc.) Arrange them on a table hidden from view. Explain that the objective is to work together to recognize the objects which will be used on the job. Give each team one minute to view objects in silence. When groups have returned to tables, have individuals write all they can remember in two minutes. Have a recorder make a "Master List" to demonstrate that teamwork gets better results than working alone. This game works well for employee orientation or retraining crossfunctional groups.

MATERIALS
REQUIRED: Number and type of objects depends on program.

APPROXIMATE
TIME REQUIRED: 25 minutes.

SOURCE: Susan Blouch and Beth Summers, Taubman Companies, Bloomfield, MI.

IX.

SELF-CONCEPT

POSITIVE STROKES

OBJECTIVE: To have the participants go home with positive affirmations. Primarily designed for workshop sessions (25 or fewer participants).

PROCEDURE: Two or three times during the session, each person fills out a 3 x 5 card about other participants, completing sentences such as THE THING I LIKE BEST ABOUT (name) IS. Or, THE BIGGEST IMPROVEMENT I SAW IN (name) IS. At the end of the day, the folded cards are passed out and read aloud and then given to the named person. He/she then goes home with 15 to 25 positive affirmations.

MATERIALS REQUIRED: 3 x 5 index cards.

APPROXIMATE TIME REQUIRED: 15 minutes.

SOURCE: Bob Bloch, Lenox. MA.

YOU'RE OK!

OBJECTIVE: To ensure closing a seminar on a positive note.

PROCEDURE: Distribute a 3 x 5 (or larger) index card to each participant toward the end of the half-day (or longer) seminar. Each person writes his/her name on the 3 x 5 or 4 x 6 index cards (top line of the card.) Cards are passed around group, at which time everyone jots one positive comment about the respective individuals. The filled cards are returned to each person.

MATERIALS REQUIRED: 3 x 5 or 4 x 6 index cards.

APPROXIMATE TIME REQUIRED: 15-20 minutes.

SOURCE: Unknown.

CONFRONTING THE BEAR

OBJECTIVE: To show that obstacles can be overcome. Designed for use in programs dealing with self-image or interpersonal skills.

PROCEDURE: Seminar leader describes a scene of walking alone in a forest and meeting a bear. Audience is asked to give one-word responses as to what they would do in the situation. Leader records those responses on a flip chart or an overhead projector. Leader then reveals that the answers given are also how we respond to the "bears" we meet everyday, the problems we face on a daily basis.

It is an excellent learning technique for self-image analyzing and provides a very positive and entertaining exercise.

MATERIALS
REQUIRED: Flip chart or overhead projector.

APPROXIMATE
TIME REQUIRED: 10 minutes.

SOURCE: Bill Edwards, Greenville, OH.

THE ONE-MINUTE PRAISE

OBJECTIVE: To give participants some positive feedback.

PROCEDURE: Describe the importance of positive stroking for behavior modification. Dr. Ken Blanchard (The One Minute Manager) suggests we "catch people doing something right." To quote Lord Chesterfield's advice: "Make a person like himself/herself a little better and I promise he/she will like you very well indeed."

Tell participants you're going to ask them to do something they may find awkward or even embarrassing. Ask them each to turn to the person next to them and say something nice to that person about that person (i.e., a "one-minute praise").

DISCUSSION QUESTIONS: (After activity) "How do you feel right now? (Most will acknowledge a positive reaction.)

How many of you--having been given that perhaps embarrassing assignment--turned to the person on your left or right (pause) smiled (pause) and said "You go first?"

When was the last time someone gave you an honest compliment?

More importantly, when was the last time you gave someone else a word of praise?

MATERIALS REQUIRED: None.

APPROXIMATE TIME REQUIRED: Three-five minutes.

SOURCE: Adapted from "The One Minute Manager", Ken Blanchard.

PEAK PERFORMANCE

OBJECTIVE: To allow participants to identify a specific activity or incident that was a "Peak Performance."

PROCEDURE: In a discussion of "excellence" or "quality service" (or other relevant topics), comment that we've all experienced those "special moments" of a peak performance. Divide into groups (3-4 to a group) and ask each participant to tell others of a recent such incident. Each group selects one person to report his/her peak performance to the entire group.

MATERIALS REQUIRED: None.

APPROXIMATE TIME REQUIRED: 15-20 minutes.

SOURCE: Unknown.

X.

TEAM BUILDING

LET'S STRING ALONG

OBJECTIVE: To demonstrate the interdependency of individuals.

PROCEDURE: Start by stressing that we are all dependent on others. To illustrate your point, ask group members who they are dependent on in that group. The first person is given a ball of string and picks out someone s/he works with. The person throws the ball at the co-worker, and states the nature of that dependency. Continue process as time permits. If the entire group is "tied" together restate and restress the initial point.

DISCUSSION QUESTIONS: Even with the independent nature of our jobs, most of us still need others. Why?

How did you choose the person to whom you tossed the ball of string? Could there have been others?

Can you think of any cases where we operate totally without support?

MATERIALS REQUIRED: Balls of string.

APPROXIMATE TIME REQUIRED: 15-20 minutes.

SOURCE: Unknown.

A COAT OF ARMS

OBJECTIVE: To give participants the opportunity to describe qualities about themselves and to learn more about other attendees.

PROCEDURE: Reproduce the coat of arms as illustrated on page 291, or ask participants to draw a similar sketch.

In space 1, draw something that characterizes a recent "Peak Performance."

In space 2, sketch out something about yourself that very few people know.

Draw in space 3 a symbol of how you like to spend your spare time.
For space 4, fill in something you really are very good at.
In space 5, write or draw something that epitomizes your personal motto.

After each person finishes, form triads (preferably of attendees who don't know each other), and try to identify what the others' coats of arms signify.

Ask for several participants to describe their coats of arms to the group.

MATERIALS
REQUIRED: None.

APPROXIMATE
TIME REQUIRED: 15-20 minutes.

SOURCE: Varied.

COAT OF ARMS

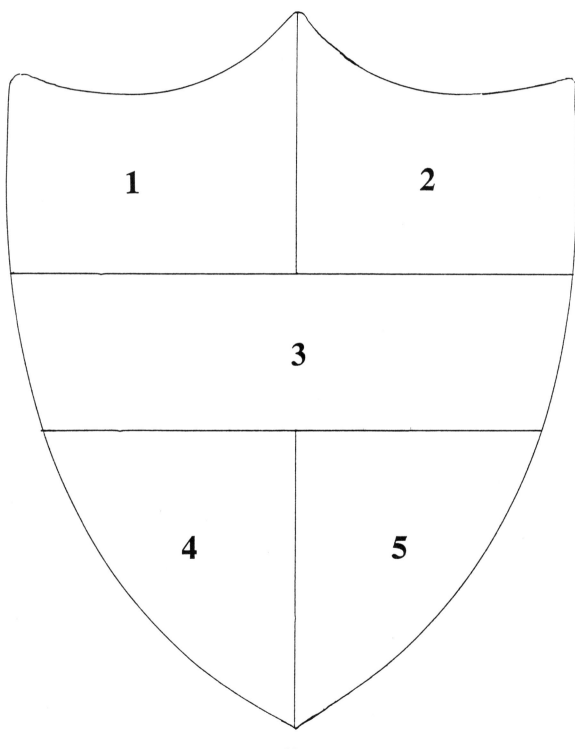

WHAT'S IN (ON) A PENNY?

OBJECTIVE: To highlight value of group (team) efforts; to demonstrate the importance of details.

PROCEDURE: Ask participants, working individually, to list all the distinguishable characteristics of a common penny.

Divide the participants into groups. Have them share their lists, check them for accuracy, and by brainstorming develop a new master list of characteristics.

Have them compare their individual and group lists with the master list (and/or the visual sketch) provided.

a.   Record, through a show of hands, how many individuals scored each item correctly.

b.   Record, through a show of hands of a spokesperson from each group, how many groups scored each item correctly.

c.   Compute the average individual score and the average group score.

DISCUSSION QUESTIONS: What does this tell you about the value of team (at least of pooled individuals) efforts?

What methods could be used to increase trainers' attention to important details for better recall of items?

How can individuals see almost daily something as common as a penny yet not "see " its characteristics?

To what degree is it true in your jobs that "it's the little things (like forgotten characteristics of a penny) that will get you"?

MATERIALS REQUIRED: None, other than a list of characteristics and/or visual diagram of a penny to provide a visual standard to compare results against.

APPROXIMATE TIME REQUIRED: 15 minutes.

SOURCE: Unknown.

FRONT VIEW

BACK VIEW

FEATURES OF A PENNY

FRONT SIDE:

1. "IN GOD WE TRUST"

2. "LIBERTY"

3. DATE

4. MINT MARK (under date, sometimes)

5. PRESIDENT LINCOLN'S PORTRAIT

BACK SIDE:

6. "UNITED STATES OF AMERICA"

7. "ONE CENT"

8. "E PLURIBUS UNUM"

9. LINCOLN MEMORIAL (12 columns)

GENERAL:

10. COPPER COLORED

11. RAISED RIM AROUND EDGE ON BOTH SIDES

12. FRONT AND BACK ARE INVERTED FROM EACH OTHER

13. DIAMETER IS 3/4 OF AN INCH

14. THICKNESS IS APPROXIMATELY 1/16 OF AN INCH

15. WEIGHT IS APPROXIMATELY 1/6 OUNCE

ZAP! YOU'RE A GROUP!

OBJECTIVE: To speed the development of working groups within a training session.

To demonstrate issues related to the group dynamics, team building, problem solving, time-management, organization, and leadership under a severe time constraint.

PROCEDURE: Begin the session by announcing that groups are to work on a specific task for the next __ minutes (e.g., 30 minutes). By the conclusion of the time period, they need to present a written report summarizing their conclusions. They may organize in any fashion they wish.

Present them with a task of your choice, preferably one that is organizationally or societally relevant or job related. (An example might be to "brainstorm various ways to reduce the turnover in our company by 10% within the next 90 days," or to "suggest ways in which we could substantially improve customer service.") Answer any procedural questions they may have, provide them with a word processor or typewriter, and walk away (to a place where you can observe and listen, but not interact).

DISCUSSION QUESTIONS: Who emerged as the leader? Why?

Who played what other roles within the group? What other roles needed to be played but received low priority?

What problems did the group encounter? How were they overcome? How could they be handled differently?

What was the effect of severe time pressure on the group's motivation? On its ultimate productivity? What about the absence (nonparticipance) of the trainer?

MATERIALS REQUIRED: None, unless a written statement of the problem and its background is desired. However, this is not designed as a case study, and therefore does not require the same level of supporting materials.

APPROXIMATE
TIME REQUIRED: From 15 minutes to an hour, depending on the task, time availability, and expectation of written product.

SOURCE: Dr. Barry Armandi, SUNY-Old Westbury, NY.

WHAT'S OUR NAME? LOGO? SLOGAN?

OBJECTIVE: To allow task groups the opportunity to develop working relationships before confronting their "real" tasks.

PROCEDURE: Form participants into small groups that they will stay with for the duration of the workshop. Allow them a few minutes to meet and introduce themselves.

Ask each group to select a simple team name in the next five minutes.

Ask them to develop a graphic logo (trademark) that will usefully portray who/what they are to the rest of the world. Allow 10 minutes for this activity, and then ask each group to show their product to the others, with a brief explanation of what the logo represents (if it is not clear). The logos should be drawn on the flip chart paper.

Then ask each group to develop a slogan (e.g., 12 words or less) that they could use in public advertising. This slogan should identify whatever assets or attributes the group realistically thinks are most important, and present within themselves. Allow 10 minutes for this activity, and then ask each group to verbally share their slogan with the others.

DISCUSSION QUESTIONS: Whose name is best? Which logo is best? Whose advertising slogan is best? What criteria are you using to judge the quality of each of those three tasks?

How do you now feel about your group? Will it be successful in its future tasks? Will it be personally satisfying to work in it?

What is the value of spending some time creating group identity at the start of a task group? What is the cost?

MATERIALS REQUIRED: Flip chart paper and markers for each group.

APPROXIMATE TIME REQUIRED: 30 minutes.

SOURCE: D. D. Warrick, Colorado Springs, CO.

TRUST ME

OBJECTIVE: To demonstrate teamwork for support, leadership, and cooperation.

PROCEDURE: Divide group into teams of four. Participation should be voluntary. One person in each group is blindfolded, another is the leader who will instruct the blindfolded person to go from Point A to Point B in the room or adjacent area. The other two persons assist the leader and make certain the blindfolded person doesn't bump into anything. When the walk (two-three minutes) is completed, switch roles and repeat the exercise using a different route. Repeat as time allows.

DISCUSSION QUESTIONS:

How did you feel when blindfolded? (Uncertain, frightened, dumb, etc.)

Did you trust your leader? Why or why not?

Did you trust your co-workers? Why or why not?

What did you need when you were blindfolded? (Support, assurance, advice, etc.)

How did this activity apply to our organization? (Need help, counsel, affirmation, etc.)

How about our new employees?

MATERIALS REQUIRED: Bandanas.

APPROXIMATE TIME REQUIRED: 20-30 minutes.

SOURCE: Susan Mitchell, Barclays Bank, Poughkeepsie, NY.

WHAT DO I (WE) WANT IN LIFE?

OBJECTIVE: To provide opportunity for individual goal clarification and goal setting.

To provide a team-building opportunity through the sharing of key personal values.

To provide teams with a task to work on as a vehicle for assessing and improving their process skills.

PROCEDURE: Provide all participants with a copy of the "What Are My Values?" form (see page 307), and ask them to complete it individually. This may then serve as the first step in personal goal clarification/goal setting.

Form participants into small groups (e.g., five persons). Ask them to share their individual rankings and arrive at a group consensus of the rankings that the typical American would provide.

When they are completed, share the "key" with them (for Column 3), and let them compute a measure of their similarity/dissimilarity to other Americans by calculating the sum of the absolute arithmetic differences (e.g., without regard to +/- sign) between their individual rankings and the key (Column 1), and between their group rankings and the key (Column 5).

DISCUSSION QUESTIONS: What are the possible reasons for the differences in rankings observed?

What are the implications of your own rankings?

MATERIALS REQUIRED: Enough individual sheets for each participant, visual key.

APPROXIMATE TIME REQUIRED: 15-60 minutes, depending on use for Objective #1, vs. 2 & 3.

SOURCE: Adapted from Sandra J. Ball-Rokeach, Milton Rokeach, and Joel W. Grube, "The Great American Values Test," Psychology Today, November 1984.

WHAT DO I (WE) WANT IN LIFE?

What Are My Values?

DIRECTIONS: Examine each of the following items. Rank-order them, in column 2, from 1-9 (1=highest priority; 9=lowest) according to the priority you would place on achieving them. Later, if small groups are formed, discuss the items with other participants and arrive at a consensus ranking in column 4 for the priority order in which you feel the typical American would rank them.

VALUE	1 Ind. Diff.	2 Indiv.	3 Key	4 Group	5 Diff.
An Exciting Life					
A Sense of Accomplishment					
A World of Beauty					
Family Security					
Freedom					
Happiness					
Inner Harmony					
National Security					
True Friendship					

TOTALS

KEY TO VALUES EXERCISE

VALUE	AMERICANS' RANK
AN EXCITING LIFE	9
A SENSE OF ACCOMPLISHMENT	4
A WORLD OF BEAUTY	8
FAMILY SECURITY	1
FREEDOM	2
HAPPINESS	3
INNER HARMONY	6
NATIONAL SECURITY	7
TRUE FRIENDSHIP	5

HELP WANTED

In a continuing effort to share the hundreds of exercises, activities and games used by trainers, speakers and meeting planners, we'd like to solicit your assistance. If you've developed an original activity, or have used one that might be shared with your colleagues, we'd appreciate hearing about it.

You can use this form (make copies if needed) and send it in. If you can help identify the source or originator, we can research it from that point. Thank You!

TITLE: _____

OBJECTIVE: _____

_____

PROCEDURE: _____

_____

_____

_____

_____

_____

_____

_____

_____

**MATERIALS
REQUIRED:** _____

**APPROXIMATE
TIME REQUIRED:** _____

SOURCE: _____

Please return to: Edward E. Scannell, Director, University Conference Bureau, Arizona State University, Tempe, Arizona 85287-1708 or John Newstrom, School of Business & Economics 110, University of Minnesota-Duluth, Minnesota 55812.